A Hustler's Journey - Against The Shadow

Deception, Volume 1

Willy Lapse Laguerre

Published by Willy Lapse Laguerre, 2024.

While every precaution has been taken in the preparation of this book, the publisher assumes no responsibility for errors or omissions, or for damages resulting from the use of the information contained herein.

A HUSTLER'S JOURNEY - AGAINST THE SHADOW

First edition. November 11, 2024.

Copyright © 2024 Willy Lapse Laguerre.

ISBN: 979-8224032778

Written by Willy Lapse Laguerre.

Also by Willy Lapse Laguerre

Cultural Differences
The Forbidden Love

Deception
A Hustler's Journey - Against The Shadow

Fairy Tales Story
The King of Milk Tome 1
The Child Of Shadows

Poetry
Where The Shadow Can not Reach

Relationship
The Game You Can Never Win

The Shattered Veil
The Valley Of The Masks

Thriller Horror
Station 13

Table of Contents

Foreword 1
ACKNOWLEDGMENTS 5
Chapter 1 | The Arrival – A Land of Promise 7
Chapter 2 | Roots and Wings 26
Chapter 3 | The Systemic Web 39
Chapter 3 | Hustling in the Shadows 54
Chapter 4 | Shadows of Doubt 70
Chapter 5 | Light Beyond the Shadows 87
Chapter 6 | Rising in the Land of Shadows 105
Chapter 7 | The Devil's Game in the Face of Hypocrisy 118

Dedication

To those of you considering a journey like this or who may already be on the path, let me first say this: you are stronger and more capable than you might imagine. Choosing to build a life in a new country is one of the bravest, most challenging things a person can do. You'll face moments of doubt, frustration, and uncertainty, but you'll also find strength, resilience, and joy in places you never expected. This advice is for you, the future hustlers, the dreamers, and the doers as you forge your path.

Foreword

THE JOURNEY OF BUILDING a new life in a foreign land is not just a story of personal growth—it's a testament to the human spirit's boundless resilience, adaptability, and hope. As you turn these pages, you'll be invited into a world of challenges, triumphs, setbacks, and hard-won wisdom. This book is more than just a memoir; it's a roadmap, a legacy, and a message of encouragement to anyone who has ever dared to dream beyond their current circumstances. I could never have imagined the path ahead when I began this journey. Leaving behind the familiar to start fresh in a country filled with opportunities but also immense challenges was a decision that came with great excitement and deep uncertainty. Germany promised stability, security, and a chance to build a future. Yet, it also came with obstacles that sometimes made me question if the dream I held was truly within reach. The idea to write this book was born out of a desire to share my experiences openly without whitewashing the difficulties or downplaying the triumphs. For those who may be on a similar path or considering a journey of their own, I wanted to offer not just my story, but insights, reflections, and practical advice that could serve as both a source of guidance and a source of strength. Each chapter represents a chapter of my own life, moments of struggle and resilience that taught me lessons I never would have learned if I had stayed within the comfort of the familiar. In Germany, I learned that the path to success is rarely straightforward. For many foreigners, the journey is marked by paradoxes: opportunity intertwined with struggle, acceptance tempered by isolation, and progress shadowed by setbacks.

This duality—the ability to hold both light and shadow, joy and sorrow, hope and uncertainty—became a central theme in my life and, ultimately, in this book. I came to see each challenge not as a barrier, but as a teacher, an opportunity to dig deeper into myself and to discover strengths I never knew I had. Through my story, I hope to shed light on the realities of building a life in a new country, particularly in a society where foreigners often face economic, social, and cultural hurdles. From language barriers to the complexities of bureaucracy, from finding work to building a sense of belonging, each experience has been both a challenge and a catalyst for growth. But this book is not just about the struggles; it's about the resilience that emerges from them, the power of persistence, and the beauty of creating a life filled with purpose and meaning. One of the most transformative lessons I learned was the importance of adaptability. In a new environment, adaptability becomes more than just a skill—it's a survival tool, a way of bending without breaking, of finding new paths when the original one is blocked. Adaptability allowed me to adjust my goals, to shift my perspective, and to embrace the unexpected. It taught me that success is not always about following a straight line, but finding strength in flexibility and viewing each detour as an opportunity rather than a setback. Community also played a critical role in my journey. In the foreign community, I found a network of people who understood my struggles, had faced similar challenges, and were willing to offer support and guidance. These connections became my lifeline, a source of encouragement on days when the path felt too difficult to continue. I discovered that we are not meant to walk this journey alone, that our strength often comes from the people who stand beside us, share our experiences, and celebrate our victories, no matter how small. The community we build with others is, in many ways, a legacy we leave behind, a gift to future generations who will benefit from the paths we have forged together. In these pages, you'll find my story and the wisdom gained from a lifetime of learning, adapting, and growing.

I share the lessons I learned in the hopes that they might resonate with you that they might offer guidance as you navigate your own challenges, whether they are similar to mine or entirely unique. This book is a reminder that resilience is not just about surviving; it's about thriving, about creating a life that affects both your dreams and your reality. One of the themes that I explore throughout this book is the idea of legacy—the impact we have on those who come after us, the ways in which our journey creates a foundation for future generations. For many of us, building a life in a new country is not just about personal success; it's about leaving a trail for others to follow, about creating a path that makes it easier for those who come after us. This legacy is a gift, a testament to the power of persistence and the importance of community. Each lesson learned, each struggle overcome, becomes a part of that legacy, a contribution to a brighter, more inclusive future. In writing this book, I was also inspired by the younger generations, by those who are just beginning to dream of lives that are different, perhaps even greater, than the ones they know. To them, I hope this book serves as a message of encouragement, a reminder that dreams are worth pursuing, that the challenges you face are not insurmountable, and that every step forward is a testament to your strength. The journey may not be easy, but it is filled with meaning, growth, and endless possibilities. This book is also a call to action. It's an invitation to each reader to embrace their own journey and recognize that challenges are not merely obstacles but opportunities for growth. It's a reminder that within each of us is a wellspring of resilience, a strength that can carry us through the darkest times, and that with patience, persistence, and adaptability, we can build lives of purpose, stability, and joy. As you read through these pages, I hope you find not only inspiration but practical insights, stories that resonate with your own experiences, and reminders that you are not alone on this journey. I hope my story encourages you to see your path with new eyes, embrace the challenges, celebrate each victory, and believe in your potential to create a life rich with meaning and possibility. No matter where you are in your journey—whether you're just beginning, somewhere in the middle, or reflecting back on years of experience—I hope you find value in the lessons shared here. Each word, each reflection, each lesson in this book comes from a place of deep honesty, resilience, and hope. It is a story of persistence, a testament to the power of community, and a reminder that we can create change for ourselves and those who come after us. In the shadows, I found the strength to rise, and it is my hope that this book helps you find your own strength, your own resilience, and your own path to a life that is both fulfilling and impactful. Thank you for embarking on this journey with me. I hope that, together, we can continue to build a world where everyone, regardless of where they come from, can find a place to belong, thrive, and call home.

ACKNOWLEDGMENTS

WRITING THIS BOOK HAS been a journey as profound as the experiences it describes, and I am immensely grateful for the people who have been by my side through it all. This book would not have been possible without their support, encouragement, and guidance. To my family: Thank you for being my anchor. You have been my inspiration, strength, and unwavering love source. Your encouragement has regenerated my dreams, even when the path was unclear. Thank you for believing in me and supporting me as I navigated new lands and challenges. Your faith in me has been the foundation of everything I've accomplished. To my friends and mentors: You have been my guiding light. Each of you has played a unique role in my journey, offering wisdom, laughter, and a shoulder to lean on during difficult times. Your advice and insights have shaped my perspective and helped me become who I am today. Thank you for sharing your experiences, lending me strength when needed, and walking with me on this journey. To the foreign community in Germany: Thank you for showing me the true meaning of resilience, unity, and solidarity. Together, we have faced challenges, celebrated victories, and built a network of support that has become a lifeline for so many of us. You have been my extended family in a land far from home, and I am grateful for every connection, every shared meal, and every word of encouragement. This book is, in many ways, a tribute to our collective strength. To my readers: Thank you for embarking on this journey with me. I hope that these pages bring you inspiration, comfort, and encouragement. Writing this book was as much an act of reflection as it was an offering to you—a testament to the power of resilience and the possibility of creating a meaningful life no matter where we are. Thank you for allowing my story to become a part of your journey. And finally, to everyone who dreams of building a life in a new land: This book is dedicated to you. I hope my story serves as a reminder that you are not alone, that every challenge can be overcome, and that every step you take creates a path for those who will follow.

Chapter 1
The Arrival – A Land of Promise

THE PLANE'S WHEELS touched down, and I felt a subtle shift—a weight lifted, only to be replaced by the unfamiliar tug of hope and apprehension. Germany, this land of precision, prosperity, and promise, stretched out before me as the plane taxied to the gate. My heart pounded with a mix of excitement and uncertainty. I had come here to carve out a new life, to hustle and make my dreams a reality. Yet, as I stepped off the plane and took my first breath of German air, I knew I was entering a different world.

The airport was a frenzy of movement—people, signs, announcements in German, and the hum of voices blending into a language I barely understood. My senses were overloaded, taking in everything, every detail. Each sign seemed like a puzzle, each word a mystery, as I navigated through customs and toward the exit. It was an unfamiliar melody, but there was an allure to it. I reminded myself that this was the beginning of a journey I had long dreamed of. Standing on foreign soil, where every corner held unknown possibilities, was intoxicating. For the first time in a long time, the weight of potential felt more substantial than that of past burdens.

Outside, the air was crisp, with the autumn chill a stark contrast to the warmth of home. The landscape was different, the skies somehow broader, inviting me to explore. I took it all in: the endless rows of well-organized streets, the precise architecture that seemed to whisper a story of progress and stability. Everything about Germany hinted at order—a place where things just worked. As a foreigner, it wasn't easy to comprehend that level of precision, but it gave me hope. If I worked hard and found my way in this structured society, maybe I could finally achieve the stability I had been chasing.

My first destination was a small apartment I had rented for the first few months. The taxi ride from the airport was an eye-opening experience. Passing meticulously clean streets, orderly traffic, and uniform buildings, I felt as if I were in a world carefully crafted and planned down to the last detail. Back home, life was vibrant, chaotic, full of movement and noise. Germany, on the other hand, seemed to breathe in harmony with itself. There was a profound sense of calm, a sense that this was a land built on discipline and purpose.

But beneath the calm, I sensed something else—a paradox I couldn't yet define. I had come here seeking a fresh start, a life free from the limitations I had known. Yet, as I observed the orderliness, a nagging thought crept in: in a land so structured, would there be room for someone like me—a hustler, a dreamer, an outsider? The excitement remained, but it mingled with a new, subtle tension, an awareness that my journey might not be as straightforward as I'd hoped.

The apartment was modest but clean, functional, and well-organized—qualities I would soon associate with German life. I unpacked my few belongings, setting each item carefully in place. This room was more than shelter; it was a space where I would gather my thoughts, refine my plans, and build the foundation for my new life. As I stood by the window that evening, looking out over the city, I felt a surge of determination. I was here now. This was real.

The first days were filled with endless tasks—registering my residence, setting up a bank account, and learning the layout of my new Cities. Simple tasks, yet each one was like a small achievement, a step toward becoming part of this society. Each interaction, whether at the bank or a grocery store, was a chance to observe and learn. People moved efficiently as if every action had a purpose. There was no rush, yet there was no wasted time. I realized I was stepping into a culture where discipline was woven into the fabric of daily life, which fascinated me.

But not everything was as smooth. Language was the first hurdle. I had picked up a few German phrases before arriving, enough to get by, but navigating a foreign language daily was overwhelming. I would listen carefully, trying to catch the rhythm of the conversations around me, hoping to make sense of words and expressions. The language barrier was a reminder that I was, in every way, an outsider here. It was humbling but also motivating. I might truly belong if I could conquer this language and speak and understand it fluently.

In those early days, I became acutely aware of the paradox of my new life in Germany. This was a land of opportunity, where hard work and discipline could open doors. But it was also a land where the barriers were invisible yet palpable. The bureaucratic systems, the unspoken rules, and the social structures would require understanding and adaptation. To succeed here, I must master the language and the culture. I was prepared to work, but I saw that this journey would demand more than effort. It would require patience, resilience, and navigating a society not made for outsiders.

As days turned into weeks, I started to appreciate the beauty of Germany's way of life—the efficiency, the focus on quality, the balance between work and leisure. People here respected time and structure in a way I hadn't seen before. Shops closed early, Sundays were sacred and quiet, and there was a sense of rhythm in daily routines. This order was comforting, a sign that life here followed rules that made sense. And yet, beneath that surface, I felt the weight of being foreign. No matter how much I admired German culture, I was constantly aware of my status as an outsider, trying to find a place in a world that seemed to value stability over change.

One evening, while walking through the city, I passed by a bustling café and caught a glimpse of people gathered, laughing, talking with ease. The warmth inside, the sense of belonging, struck me deeply. I realized that beyond economic stability, I longed for connection, for a sense of being part of this society. But I also knew that I was in for a long journey. Integrating here would require more than learning the language or adapting to customs—it would require a transformation, a shift in how I saw myself and my place in the world.

Germany had welcomed me with the promise of opportunity, but it was clear that this promise came with conditions. To succeed, I would need to adapt without losing myself, to find a balance between who I was and who I needed to become to thrive in this structured land. This was a place where discipline and perseverance were valued, and I would need to harness those qualities within myself to overcome the challenges ahead.

In those quiet moments of reflection, I made a promise to myself as I looked out at the city lights. No matter how difficult the journey, I would not give up. I had come here to build a better life and was prepared to fight for it. I knew this land of promise held light and shadow, but I was determined to navigate both. Germany would be my proving ground, where I would test my limits, face my fears, and pursue my dreams with unwavering determination.

The journey had only begun, but I felt a deep sense of purpose in that moment. I was ready to embrace the paradox, to walk the line between opportunity and obstacle. With all its order and structure, Germany had become my new home, where I would learn, grow, and, one day, thrive.

The Land of Stability, The Struggle of Belonging

Germany is, in many ways, a marvel of modern stability. The economy, built on a foundation of engineering prowess, meticulous planning, and a robust social system, is often seen as an economic miracle, a model of resilience that weathered financial storms that shook other nations. Germany represents a safe harbor for outsiders, especially those from less stable countries. In this place, rules are clear, opportunities exist for those willing to work, and a sense of order permeates everything. But hidden beneath this surface of opportunity is a complex reality: for foreigners, carving out a space within this stable society can be an uphill struggle, a battle against invisible barriers that challenge one's finances, identity, and sense of belonging.

When I first arrived, the prosperity was unmistakable. Everywhere I looked, I saw signs of a well-oiled system—clean streets, efficient public transportation, orderly lines, and a pace of life that seemed disciplined and relaxed. It felt like I had entered a world where life's rhythm was set to a steady, reliable beat. The Germans around me went about their daily lives with a sense of calm that I found both admirable and foreign. It was a place where things worked; the systems were predictable, the structures unwavering, and the rules adhered to with precision.

Yet, as a foreigner, I quickly learned that this stability was not as accessible as it appeared from the outside. It became clear that while Germany's economic engine was open to skilled workers and hardworking immigrants, the road to stability for foreigners was lined with invisible obstacles. Despite being in a country known for its inclusivity and opportunities, I grappled with an unsettling reality: stability here seemed attainable only for those who fit within specific frameworks, those who could mingle themselves to fit the systems in place. For those from different backgrounds who spoke other languages or brought unique perspectives, the pathway to belonging was fraught with challenges.

The paradox became even more pronounced as I interacted with other foreigners in Germany. Many of us had come here for similar reasons—to escape instability, build a better life, and find security in a land where economic hardships were supposedly less pressing. However, the reality was that while Germany's economy was stable, the system was far from welcoming. The requirements for inclusion were clear-cut but challenging to meet. Finding a job, securing housing, or even understanding the layers of bureaucracy felt like a series of tests that few passed without a struggle.

One of the first hurdles was the language. While many Germans spoke English, mastering German was essential to gaining access to better jobs and integrating more fully into society. For newcomers, however, the language barrier became a defining factor that immediately separated us from locals. Despite our qualifications, skills, and determination, many of us were limited to jobs that didn't require fluent German. The paradox was evident: in a country built on precision, our inability to meet the language standard meant our qualifications often went unrecognized, leaving us to settle for positions far below our potential.

This struggle was magnified when it came to navigating Germany's bureaucratic labyrinth. Every step of establishing oneself—registering a residence, opening a bank account, obtaining health insurance—required a level of familiarity with the language and the system that was daunting for newcomers. Each form, appointment, and piece of paper reminded me of the gap between the life I envisioned and the reality I was facing. For many Germans, these were simple tasks, part of the natural rhythm of life. However, each requirement was a test of resilience and patience for foreigners, and every misstep felt like a setback in an otherwise efficient system.

The paradox of stability extended into the job market as well. Germany's economy is renowned for its strength and demand for skilled workers, especially in fields like engineering, technology, and healthcare. Yet, despite this demand, foreigners often find themselves sidelined, struggling to gain recognition for their credentials and skills. Many immigrants come with qualifications that would be highly regarded in their home countries. However, foreign degrees and certifications are often scrutinized and sometimes discounted in Germany. I met doctors who were driving taxis, engineers who were cleaning buildings, and teachers who were working in kitchens. The opportunity was there, tantalizingly close, yet the path to access it seemed guarded by gatekeepers who required a level of conformity that was out of reach for many.

This lack of recognition extended beyond professional life and seeped into social interactions. While Germany's stability was built on mutual respect and order, I began to see how the same order maintained in this society could also act as a barrier for those trying to fit in. An unspoken code, a set of cultural expectations, defined what it meant to be "German." For foreigners, especially those from non-European backgrounds, fitting into this shape was challenging. Our accents, our cultural differences, our ways of interacting—all of these marked us as "other," reminding us that, despite our efforts, we were still outsiders.

One aspect that stood out was the difficulty in securing housing. Germany's housing market is notoriously competitive, but the challenges are amplified for foreigners. Landlords often preferred tenants with a stable job history in Germany, a flawless credit score, and references from previous landlords—all things newcomers didn't have. Many ended up in temporary accommodations, sublets, or less desirable Area. We were caught in a paradox where the stability of German society seemed closed off, with the housing market acting as a gatekeeper that silently but firmly maintained the divide.

Another subtle barrier was the German value of stability itself. In Germany, stability is not only an economic reality but a cultural expectation. People plan for the long term; they value security, predictability, and rootedness. For foreigners, many of whom come from places where life is more transient or unpredictable, adapting to this cultural norm requires a shift in mindset. I often felt like I was on a quest for survival and growth, while my German counterparts seemed content to build on foundations already laid. This cultural difference created an unspoken divide, a feeling that, as much as I respected and admired German stability, my approach to life was inherently different.

Yet, despite these challenges, something was inspiring about Germany's stability. It was a double-edged sword—sometimes frustrating and a source of hope. Germany represented a land where dreams could come true, but only if one navigated its complexities. I saw other foreigners, people from all walks of life, hustling, adapting, and finding creative ways to carve out a space for themselves. Some started small businesses, those who found a niche in the job market, and those who, through sheer determination, managed to integrate and build a life. Each story was a testament to resilience, a reminder that even in a land where unyielding structures guard stability, there is room for growth and opportunity.

In these interactions with fellow foreigners, I found a sense of solidarity. We were all aware of the paradox—this was a land of promise, but the promises were conditional, accessible only to those who could adapt and navigate the barriers. We shared stories, exchanged advice, and supported each other. We were working to survive and strive to thrive, to make Germany a place where we could feel at home, even if the journey was challenging.

The longer I stayed, the more I saw how the stability of Germany created both opportunity and exclusion. It was a system that worked seamlessly for those who fit into it, but for outsiders; it was a world of hoops to jump through and barriers to overcome. I often considered Germany a grand symphony, where every note was carefully placed, every instrument played in harmony. But for foreigners, it was as if we were handed a different sheet of music, left to find our place within a melody that didn't naturally accommodate us.

Looking back, I realized that the struggles foreigners face in Germany are not just about economics or bureaucracy but about identity and belonging. The challenge is not only to build a life here but to find a way to bridge the gap between one's own culture and the structured rhythms of German society. It is a journey of adaptation, of learning to exist within a paradox where opportunity and exclusion coexist.

In a way, the hidden struggles are what give depth to this land of promise. They test the resolve of those who come here, pushing us to grow in ways we hadn't anticipated. With all its economic stability and unspoken rules, Germany taught me the value of resilience, the importance of adaptability, and the power of community. For in the face of these challenges, the sense of belonging we create is hard-earned, and the spaces we carve out for ourselves become testaments to our determination.

Even the Shadow Can Rise Against You

Germany, to many, is a beacon of opportunity—a place where prosperity feels within reach, a land marked by economic stability, high living standards, and efficiency. It's a country that promises safety, order, and a chance to make a better life. Yet, as a foreigner, I found that even the shadows can rise against you in Germany. It's a metaphor for the intangible challenges, the unexpected obstacles, and the invisible forces that seem to act like shadows, casting darkness over the path just when the light appears closest.

When I first arrived, the promise of Germany was undeniable. The economy was strong, the people seemed friendly, and the opportunities, from the outside, appeared abundant. I saw a future in this place—a stable job, a secure home, a life of dignity and growth. But as I took my first steps on this journey, I quickly realized that the path to opportunity was more complex. Like shadows that stretch and shift with the changing light, the obstacles here were often unseen at first glance, only to loom large when you least expected them.

In Germany, life operates on well-defined structures, a series of checks and balances that keep society running smoothly. But these structures can become barriers for anyone who doesn't fit neatly within them. As a foreigner, I felt like I was navigating a maze. I could see the exit—the promise of stability and success—but the path was obscured by walls of bureaucracy, language, and cultural expectations that seemed to block my way. It felt like walking through a city where every corner revealed a new shadow and challenge that needed to be overcome.

One of the first shadows to rise against me was the language barrier. In Germany, precision matters, clarity and understanding are paramount. Without fluent German, I felt like I was stumbling in the dark, unable to communicate or understand the nuances of conversations fully. This wasn't just about speaking—it was about comprehension and grasping the unspoken rules governing everything from workplace etiquette to everyday interactions. The language was like an invisible wall, a shadow that followed me everywhere, reminding me that I was an outsider.

Then came the bureaucratic labyrinth. Every step, from finding a place to live to opening a bank account, required navigating a system that seemed almost purposefully opaque. Forms were filled with technical terms I struggled to decipher, offices had specific hours that seemed to clash with my work schedule, and even the slightest mistake—a missed document, a wrong answer—could mean starting the entire process over again. The bureaucracy felt like a shadowy figure at my side, an ever-present reminder that my progress depended on my ability to bend every situation into my will through these convoluted processes. For locals, it was second nature, a familiar part of life. But for foreigners, the system was a test of patience and resilience, a series of invisible hurdles that had to be cleared to gain a foothold.

In the job market, the shadows were equally daunting. Germany is known for its demand for skilled workers, its respect for qualifications, and its dedication to professionalism. And yet, as a foreigner, I found that even with qualifications, the doors didn't open as quickly as I had hoped. There were unspoken expectations—certifications unfamiliar to me, job requirements that didn't align with my previous experience, and a preference for candidates who fit the "German standard." I realized that opportunity here was not always about ability or ambition but fitting into a predefined Mold. The shadow of exclusion, of not quite belonging, seemed to follow me through every interview and every job application.

Even in daily life, shadows would appear unexpectedly. Housing, for example, was an area I hadn't anticipated to be as challenging as it was. Germany has a notoriously competitive housing market, with strict requirements for tenants. Many landlords required extensive documentation—a stable job history in Germany, German references, and a high credit score—things that most foreigners didn't have. I would find a perfect apartment, only to be turned away because I lacked one or more of these requirements. The housing market was a game of shadows, a place where you could see what you wanted, but the path to securing it was hidden behind layers of criteria that seemed stacked against newcomers.

The most persistent shadow, however, was that of cultural expectation. Germany values order, stability, and tradition. While these qualities make the country strong, they can also create an unspoken standard that feels impossible to meet as a foreigner. Small things—such as knowing when and how to greet people, understanding social cues, or even knowing how to dress in a way that blended in—felt like silent judgments. But there were also more considerable expectations about work, social life, and family that seemed to set a high bar for acceptance. No one explicitly told me I didn't belong, but the shadows were in the form of glances, comments, and subtle exclusions. It was a quiet, insidious pressure, like a shadow cast by something you can't see but can always feel.

Over time, I learned that these shadows were not unique to me. I spoke with other foreigners who had come here with dreams similar to mine, only to find themselves navigating the same tangled path. Some had been here for years, still struggling to find stable housing, working jobs below their skill level, and trying to fit into a society that valued predictability over diversity. We shared stories of bureaucratic nightmares, misunderstandings in the workplace, and feeling isolated despite being surrounded by people. We were chasing the light of opportunity but were also haunted by the shadows that seemed determined to keep us from reaching it.

In moments of reflection, I began to understand the nature of these shadows. They were the product of a system that prioritized stability and valued structure over adaptability. Germany's strength—its ability to maintain a well-functioning society—was also its weakness when accepting those who didn't naturally fit. The shadows were a by-product of this system, an unintended consequence of a society that sometimes left outsiders struggling to find their place in its quest for order.

And yet, despite these challenges, I couldn't help but admire Germany. The shadows didn't diminish its promise; they made the journey more meaningful. I knew that if I could find a way through this maze and adapt and persevere, the rewards would be worth it. In a strange way, the shadows were a test of resolve, a rite of passage that separated those willing to fight for their place from those who might give up.

As time passed, I learned how to navigate these shadows. I improved my German, slowly breaking down the language barrier that had once felt insurmountable. I found ways to work within the bureaucracy, learning the system's quirks and adapting to its demands. I adjusted to the job market, taking on roles that allowed me to build experience and credibility. I even found ways to blend in culturally, learning to balance my own identity with the expectations of German society.

The shadows didn't disappear, but I learned to live with them. They became a part of my journey, a reminder of the resilience required to build a life in a land where stability comes with strings attached. Each shadow represented a challenge overcome, a lesson learned, and a step closer to achieving my envisioned life. And though the journey was difficult, it was also gratifying. I knew that every success, every small victory, was hard-earned. Each step forward felt like a triumph in a land of opportunity where the path was tangled with unseen barriers.

Ultimately, I realized that even when the shadows rise against you, they don't have to stop you. They may obscure the path, create delays, or test your patience, but they can also become part of your strength. The shadows taught me to be resourceful, to find solutions, and to embrace the journey in all its complexity. They reminded me that while Germany's opportunities are not freely given, they are there for those willing to work for them.

This understanding became the foundation of my life here. The shadows became less intimidating, less overwhelming. I stopped seeing them as obstacles and started seeing them as challenges that added depth to my journey. In a land where stability can be both a blessing and a barrier, I learned to find my light and path forward. The shadows, in their way, had shaped me, preparing me for the life I was building, a life that, despite the struggles, was filled with purpose and resilience.

A Daily Life Turned Into a Horror Catalog

In a world where appearances can dictate perceptions, your look—your skin tone, features, style, or simply the way you carry yourself—can often speak louder than words. Moving to Germany, I found that the first impression created by my appearance usually became a defining element of my daily experience, shaping interactions in ways I never expected. Despite my efforts to integrate, learn the language, and work hard to build a life, my appearance often seemed to place me in a box, a stereotype I struggled to break free from. This chapter explores the harsh reality of how appearances can become an obstacle, a constant reminder that acceptance and understanding are privileges not extended to everyonem, where every rule is set in apposition.

Every day, my appearance acted like a beacon, flagging to others that I was different. The impact of this visual identity often felt inescapable, as though I were living in an endless nightmare of prejudiced assumptions, social distancing, and quiet judgments that followed me from the workplace to the street and even into my relationships. This isn't a story of occasional glances or subtle curiosities—it's about how something as simple as how I looked could cast a shadow over every interaction, turning the most mundane moments into challenging episodes.

The First Glance: A Silent Judgment

The silent weight of being "different" began when I stepped outside. It wasn't always overt or hostile, but I was aware that I wasn't part of the default setting here. In Germany, where many people share specific physical characteristics, my presence was often noted with a glance, a double-take, or a subtle but unmistakable shift in posture from strangers. Whether on the train, in a café, or standing in line at a grocery store, I often felt the silent message, the subtle distancing.

At times, people would avoid eye contact altogether, as though acknowledging my presence would make them complicit in something uncomfortable. Other times, the gaze would linger, filled with questions I was not expected to answer but nonetheless felt obligated to. The assumptions written in their looks made clear that, for some, my appearance marked me as an outsider, someone who belonged elsewhere.

What surprised me was how quickly I became attuned to this. I could tell the difference between a glance of curiosity and one of suspicion. I could feel the weight of a stare, the way it seemed to penetrate, searching for an explanation, a reason for my presence. These judgments, delivered silently, turned simple moments into anxiety-ridden encounters, making it difficult to relax even in familiar spaces. My look had betrayed me, and there was no escape from its consequences.

In the Workplace: A Professional with an Asterisk

In professional settings, I found that my appearance could often overshadow my qualifications, experience, or skills. No matter how well I spoke, how hard I worked, or how much I adapted, my look seemed to carry its narrative—one that was not entirely within my control. This betrayal by appearance was like an asterisk next to my professional identity as if my background and appearance placed me in a different category.

In meetings, I often felt the need to prove myself twice over. Colleagues sometimes listened politely but with a certain hesitation, as though waiting to see if my ideas were worth the same consideration as others. There was an unspoken sense that I needed to validate my presence in the room to justify that I belonged there. This created an additional layer of pressure, forcing me to constantly anticipate questions and challenges others didn't have to face.

One of the most unsettling aspects was the "compliments" that sometimes came my way. I would occasionally hear things like, "You speak German so well!" or "It's impressive that you've adapted so quickly." These comments, often meant as praise, were reminders that I was viewed as an exception to the rule, a foreigner who had somehow learned to "fit in." Each well-meaning remark underscored that, in the eyes of some, I would always be an outsider, someone who had to work harder to prove my worth simply because of my appearance.

Public Spaces: Navigating Assumptions and Suspicion

In public spaces, the influence of my appearance took on another form—one that sometimes bordered on suspicion or outright discomfort. Walking down a busy street, I could sense how people would adjust their pace or cross to the other side. On public transportation, there were times when seats around me would remain empty, even when the train or bus was packed. These moments were subtle yet stinging, a constant reminder that my appearance triggered assumptions that I was somehow a threat or an anomaly.

One of the most vivid examples occurred in a small shop. I had entered to browse and was quickly approached by an employee who watched me closely, following my movements as I looked through the items. I could feel their suspicion, as though they were waiting for me to do something out of place. The scrutiny was intense and unmistakable. I left the shop without buying anything, not because I didn't want to, but because the experience made me feel uncomfortable and unwelcome. It was a small incident, but one that echoed similar encounters where my appearance alone was enough to cast doubt on my intentions.

This experience wasn't unique, and I learned to anticipate it over time. The constant vigilance from others, and the way I was sometimes made to feel like a "security risk" added a layer of anxiety to everyday life. I adjusted my attitude, making deliberate efforts to appear non-threatening to avoid any actions that might reinforce the assumptions placed on me. This self-censorship was exhausting, a constant reminder that my appearance was a barrier between myself and others.

Social Interactions: Friendships with Boundaries

My appearance also introduced complications in personal relationships, creating invisible but powerful boundaries. Making friends was not impossible, but the relationships often came with certain limitations. For some, I was the "exotic" friend, a curiosity that added diversity to their social circle but didn't fully belong. For others, I felt my friendship was conditional, limited by unspoken rules that governed how close we could become.

Sometimes, I was invited to social gatherings and introduced as an "interesting foreign friend." At first, I appreciated the invitations, grateful for the opportunity to build connections. But over time, I realized that these friendships were sometimes superficial, restricted by stereotypes and assumptions. I was often expected to "represent" my background, answer questions about my culture, and explain things others could quickly have learned on their own.

On other occasions, friendships never progressed past polite acquaintanceships. People were friendly and welcoming even, but an unspoken barrier kept me at a distance. It was as though my appearance marked me as different, and that difference was enough to keep me on the periphery. The feeling of isolation became palpable, a constant reminder that despite my efforts to integrate, there would always be those who saw me as a visitor in their world.

Law Enforcement and Authority: A Presumption of Guilt

Perhaps the most troubling aspect of my experience was how my appearance influenced encounters with law enforcement and other authorities. In situations where most people would receive neutral or courteous treatment, my look often attracted a presumption of guilt, an assumption that I was somehow up to no good.

Being stopped for ID checks or questioned without cause became an occasional part of life. These interactions were rarely aggressive, but they were unmistakably shaped by assumptions about who I was based on my appearance. Each encounter left me with a sense of vulnerability, a reminder that my rights and freedoms could be curtailed at any moment, not because of my actions, but because of how I looked.

This presumption of guilt was one of the most disheartening aspects of my experience. No matter how much I tried to prove my intentions, to present myself as harmless, there was always the risk that someone in a position of authority would view me with suspicion. It was a reminder that, in the eyes of specific individuals, my appearance was enough to warrant mistrust, that I was forever being watched and judged.

Coping with the Horror of Assumptions

Living with this constant judgment, this horror magazine of assumptions, required a level of resilience and self-awareness I had not anticipated. I had to find ways to cope with the scrutiny and manage the anxiety that came with being constantly evaluated based on my appearance. For me, this meant finding safe spaces, building friendships with people who saw beyond my exterior, and reminding myself of my worth despite the judgments of others.

I learned to focus on the positive interactions, when people treated me with kindness and openness, to counterbalance the more challenging experiences. I sought out community spaces where I could connect with others who understood my journey, shared similar struggles, and could offer understanding and solidarity. This community became my sanctuary, where I could be myself without the weight of assumptions and judgments.

Over time, I also developed a thicker skin, a way of letting the glances, the comments, and the suspicions slide off me. I learned to separate my self-worth from the opinions of others to remember that the judgments I faced reflected their biases, not my character. This mental resilience became a shield, a way of reclaiming my power in a world that often saw me only through the lens of my appearance.

A Daily Fight for Acceptance

Living in a society that judges based on appearances is a daily challenge, a fight for acceptance and understanding in a world that can be unforgiving. My look betrayed me in countless ways, turning everyday interactions into tests of resilience and courage. But through this struggle, I learned the power of self-worth, the importance of finding community, and the strength it takes to rise above stereotypes.

Chapter 2
Roots and Wings

LEAVING HOME IS A JOURNEY of contradictions—excitement and sadness, hope and trepidation. My journey from my homeland to Germany carried the weight of dreams and farewells, an experience that felt like tearing away from the familiar while reaching for something entirely unknown. Germany, to me, was a land of promise, a place that held the potential for stability, success, and growth. I carried with me the vision of a life transformed, of possibilities that felt boundless. But, like wings being stretched for the first time, the path forward would require strength, resilience, and a willingness to let go of what I once called home.

In my homeland since 1986, life has been vibrant and full of roses, but struggles have also marked it. Opportunities were scarce, and stability was a luxury that few could afford. My family, friends, and community were the pillars of my existence, but the economic challenges we faced limited our dreams. I grew up seeing people work tirelessly, their lives shaped by a constant fight to make ends meet and secure a better future for themselves and their families. My parents taught me the value of hard work, the importance of ambition, and the strength found in perseverance. As I watched them strive against the odds, I felt a desire growing within me—to break free and find a life where my efforts could lead to something more.

Germany became the symbol of that "something more." I had heard stories of its precision, of its discipline, of its unmatched economy. It was a place where hard work was rewarded, where opportunity was not a fleeting dream but a concrete reality. I wanted to build a life where I could apply my skills, expand my knowledge, and achieve financial security that had always felt out of reach. Leaving home, however, wasn't easy. It meant saying goodbye to everything that had shaped me, to the streets and faces I knew so well. But deep down, I knew that my future lay in a faraway land where I could finally stretch my wings.

Preparing to leave was a whirlwind of emotions. There were days when excitement filled me when I imagined myself walking through the streets of a new city, blending into a world of strangers who would eventually become my community. But there were also moments of doubt, of fear that perhaps I was leaving behind too much, that the bonds of home would be too difficult to replace. My family was proud yet worried; they supported my dreams but feared the unknown that awaited me. Friends told me tales of others who had gone abroad, some returning with stories of success, others with tales of struggle. Each story reminded me that the journey I was embarking on would not be simple and that dreams, no matter how hopeful, came with their challenges.

The day of my departure was bittersweet. As I hugged my family, I felt their love and hopes resting on my shoulders. My mother's eyes, filled with pride and worry, seemed to speak volumes. My father, a man of few words, patted my shoulder, his silent strength a reminder of everything he had taught me. At that moment, I understood that this journey wasn't just for me but for all of us. I was carrying my dreams and the dreams of my family, friends, and community. As I boarded the plane, I felt these dreams' weight and wings. I was leaving my roots, but I was carrying them wrapped around my heart like a protective shield.

The flight to Germany felt like a bridge between two worlds. I sat by the window, watching the land disappear beneath the clouds, feeling a sense of both loss and anticipation. I had heard that Germany was a land of opportunity, a place where hard work led to rewards, where structure and stability were part of daily life. It was a stark contrast to the uncertainty I had known back home. I imagined navigating the clean, orderly streets, working in a profession that respected my skills, and living where my future felt secure. My mind painted pictures of a life where I could finally find the balance between ambition and peace and grow without the constant fear of instability. I was filled with purpose and determination, ready to embrace the unknown.

My first glimpse of Germany was from above as the plane descended. The land looked different—clean, organized, marked by a sense of order that felt almost surreal. I was astounded by the rows of buildings, the precise layout of the roads, and the sense of calm that seemed to permeate even from the air. As we landed, I took a deep breath, feeling the weight of the journey settle upon me. This was it. I was here, in the land I had dreamed about, the place that held the promise of a better life.

Stepping off the plane, I was immediately struck by the sense of efficiency that seemed to define everything around me. The airport was a maze of signs in a language I barely understood, yet everything felt streamlined, as though every movement and action had been carefully planned. People moved with purpose, their steps steady and deliberate. It was a far cry from home's bustling, chaotic energy, and I couldn't help but feel a mix of admiration and intimidation. This was a place where precision mattered, where everything had its place, and I wondered if I would find mine here.

As I made my way through customs, I felt the first stirrings of the challenges I would face. The language was a barrier, a wall that separated me from the world around me. I had learned a few basic phrases, enough to get by, but the fluency required to communicate felt like a distant goal. I observed the people around me, their conversations flowing effortlessly in German, each word a reminder that I was, in every sense, a foreigner here. It was both humbling and motivating—a reminder that if I wanted to build a life in this land, I would need to overcome this obstacle to make this language my own.

The taxi ride to my apartment was a journey through a foreign and familiar city. I was astounded by the architecture, the clean streets, and the sense of calm that seemed to permeate everything. It was a city that radiated stability, where life seemed predictable and secure. And yet, beneath the surface, I could sense the complexity of my new world. Germany was a land of rules, unspoken expectations, and structures that provided stability and demanded conformity. I wondered if I could navigate this complex landscape to find a balance between my identity and the expectations of a society that prized order and precision.

Arriving at my apartment, I felt a surge of independence tempered by loneliness. This was my new home, where I would forge my path away from the familiarity of family and friends. I unpacked my belongings, each a reminder of the life I had left behind, each a piece of my roots. As I arranged my things, I felt a sense of both loss and liberation. This room would be my sanctuary, where I would rest, plan, and gather strength for the journey ahead. It was a blank canvas, waiting for the story I would paint with each decision, each challenge, each victory.

In the days that followed, I immersed myself in adapting. Every interaction and errand was a new experience, a chance to learn and grow. There were moments of frustration when the language barrier felt insurmountable, and the bureaucratic processes seemed designed to keep me out. But there were also moments of joy, small victories that reminded me of the strength within me. Each step forward felt like a triumph, a testament to my resilience, a reminder that I could build a life here, even if it would take time.

As I explored my new city, I reflected on the journey that had brought me here. I thought of my family, the lessons they taught me, and our shared dreams. I felt a sense of gratitude for my roots, for the strength and resilience they had instilled in me. And yet, I also felt the thrill of new wings, of the freedom to create my path and define my future. With all its challenges and promises, Germany had become my new home, where I would learn, grow, and ultimately thrive.

The journey from my homeland to Germany was marked by loss and gain, the pull of roots, and the thrill of wings. I knew that the road ahead would be difficult and that the dreams I carried would not be easily achieved. But I also knew that I was ready. I was prepared to embrace this land's promise, face the challenges, and build a life defer to my roots and new wings. This was my journey, my chance to create a life of purpose and resilience where my dreams could finally take flight.

Struggles and Surprises

Arriving in Germany felt like stepping into a world that operated on a different frequency. I was greeted by the warm smiles of immigration officers and the friendliness of locals who offered directions when I appeared lost. It was a welcoming gesture, a signal that I was entering a country that valued openness and order. But as days turned into weeks, I began to see the paradox that defined my experience here—being invited in but kept at arm's length, of being welcomed yet feeling like a permanent outsider.

One of the first struggles I encountered was the language. German is a language of precision, where every word and every syllable seems to carry its weight. While I had learned some basic phrases before arriving, the reality of daily communication hit me like a wall. Each conversation felt like a challenge, a test of my ability to navigate an unfamiliar tongue. Ordering food, asking for directions, and even simple greetings were fraught with the fear of mispronunciation, of saying something wrong. I often would find myself rehearsing phrases, trying to get the pronunciation right, only to freeze up when it was time to speak.

In those early days, every interaction was tinged with a sense of vulnerability. The locals babbled fluidly, their words flowing together in a rhythm I couldn't follow. I would listen carefully, picking out words I recognized piecing together meaning from context. But it was exhausting, a constant reminder of my status as an outsider. Sometimes, I felt like a child again, struggling to understand, express myself, and connect. I could see the patience in people's eyes the slight hesitation as they waited for me to respond. And while they were kind, I could also feel a subtle shift in their poise—a quiet reminder that, despite their welcome, I was not yet one of them.

Cultural differences added another layer of complexity. Germany is a country built on discipline, rules, and routines that guide every aspect of life. Punctuality, for example, is not just a virtue but an expectation. Back home, time was fluid, flexible, and shaped by the moment's needs. But in Germany, being late was seen as disrespectful, a breach of the unspoken code that governed interactions. I quickly learned that if I was meeting someone at ten, I needed to arrive at least five minutes early. It was a minor adjustment, yet it felt monumental, a constant reminder that I was navigating a culture that valued precision over spontaneity.

Social interactions were another surprise. Germans are reserved and often slow to warm up to new people. There was a formality in conversations, a distance that felt unfamiliar. Back home, a smile, a shared laugh, and a friendly gesture were enough to spark a connection. But here, relationships were built slowly, over time, through shared experiences and mutual respect. I longed for the easy warmth of home, the familiarity of people who understood me without explanation. Here, even casual friendships seemed to require an effort that felt foreign, a deliberate process that I struggled to understand.

One of the most challenging aspects was navigating the subtle boundaries defining every interaction. Germans value privacy, both in public and private life. Personal questions were seen as intrusive, violating the invisible barrier that protected one's personal space. Back home, asking about someone's family, work, and life was a way of showing interest and building rapport. But here, such questions were met with polite but firm responses that kept me at a distance. It was a strange feeling—to be welcomed yet held at arm's length and invited into a society where unspoken rules defined every interaction.

Housing presented its own set of struggles. Finding an apartment in Germany was like entering a competition, where the odds were often stacked against foreigners. Landlords required extensive documentation—proof of income, German credit scores, references from previous landlords—all things I didn't have. I would visit apartment after apartment, only to be turned away because I didn't meet the requirements. It was frustrating, a reminder that, despite the promise of opportunity, the path to stability was far from straightforward. Each rejection felt like a setback, a reminder that I was an outsider trying to find my place in a system that wasn't built for me.

The job market was no longer accessible. Germany's economy is renowned for its strength, demand for skilled workers, and respect for qualifications. And yet, as a foreigner, I quickly realized that my qualifications didn't hold the same weight here. Employers wanted German certifications, German experience, and German references. My skills, knowledge, and ambitions were overshadowed by a preference for candidates who fit the "German standard." I found myself applying for jobs far below my skill level, positions that felt like a step back from the dreams I had carried with me. It was a humbling experience, a reminder that, despite my determination, the path forward would require patience and adaptability.

Even in moments of success, the shadows of exclusion were ever-present. I remember my first day at a new job, a position I had fought hard to secure. My colleagues were polite and friendly, but there was an invisible barrier between us, a subtle reminder of my status as a foreigner. Conversations would shift to German, leaving me struggling to keep up and understand the jokes, the references, and the nuances. I felt both included and excluded, welcomed yet held at a distance. It was a strange, unsettling feeling—a paradox of belonging that left me constantly aware of my outsider status.

There were moments of loneliness, times when the weight of these struggles felt overwhelming. I would walk through the city, surrounded by people, yet feeling isolated and disconnected from the world around me. The language barrier, the cultural differences, and the unspoken rules combined to create a sense of distance that I couldn't bridge. It was a reminder that, despite the opportunities, despite the promise, the path to belonging in Germany was fraught with invisible hurdles, with shadows that seemed determined to remind me of my place on the margins.

And yet, amidst these struggles, there were moments of surprise—small acts of kindness, gestures that reminded me that, beneath the barriers, there was a shared humanity. A stranger is offering directions with a smile, a colleague patiently explaining a task in English, and a landlord who gave me a chance despite my lack of references. These moments were like rays of light breaking through the shadows, reminders that the journey was not in vain despite the challenges; there was hope.

Over time, I began to see the paradox of my experience in Germany more clearly. This country valued order, structure, and stability—where everything had its place, rules were followed, and expectations were clear. But it was also a country that, in its pursuit of precision, often left little room for those who didn't fit the frame. As a foreigner, I was welcomed and excluded, invited in, but kept at a distance. The struggle was not only to find my place but to redefine what belonging meant in a society that valued conformity over diversity.

Looking back, I realized that these early struggles were shaping me, teaching me lessons that would become the foundation of my journey. I was learning to navigate the language, adapt to the cultural expectations, and find my path in a welcoming and unyielding society. Each challenge and moment of exclusion reminded me of my resilience to adapt, persevere, and find strength in adversity.

The struggles and surprises of those early days became a part of my story, a reminder that, in Germany, even the shadows could rise against you. But they also taught me that, despite the challenges, the promise of this land was still within reach. The path was not easy, but it was worth taking, a journey that would test my limits, shape my character, and ultimately lead me to a life of purpose and resilience.

Determination

Determination is a quiet force, a resolve that builds within you, often unnoticed, until it becomes the fuel that drives you forward. In those early days in Germany, I came face-to-face with challenges that tested my resolve in ways I hadn't anticipated, and each day brought new hurdles, from language struggles to cultural misunderstandings, from the weight of bureaucracy to the constant reminder that I was an outsider. But beneath it all, I felt a growing determination, a resolve to carve out a space for myself, to succeed in a country that welcomed me and held me at arm's length.

The first step was to adjust and find a rhythm within the structured pace of German life. I quickly realized that if I wanted to succeed, I would have to learn to blend in and adapt without losing myself. I studied the routines of those around me, observing their habits, ways of interacting, and unspoken rules. I watched how people greeted each other with a polite nod, how they valued punctuality, and how they kept their personal lives private, even in friendly conversations. It was a different world from the one I had known, but I was determined to learn, understand, and adapt.

The language barrier, however, remained one of the biggest obstacles. Every day, I would practice my German, repeating phrases, memorizing vocabulary, and trying to understand the nuances that seemed to escape me. I signed up for language classes, determined to break through the wall that separated me from full participation in German society. The classes were challenging, filled with other foreigners equally determined to learn and integrate. We shared a common goal: a shared understanding of our struggles. And in those classes, I found a sense of camaraderie, a reminder that I was not alone in this journey.

Outside of class, I immersed myself in the language wherever I could. I would listen to German radio stations, watch German television, and read street signs, all to train my ears to the sounds and rhythms of the language. I would practice speaking with strangers, even if it meant stumbling over my words or facing the occasional look of impatience or confusion. Each interaction, each small victory, was a step forward, a reminder that progress was possible. My determination to overcome the language barrier became a daily mantra, a promise to myself that I would not let this obstacle define me.

But language was only one part of the equation. The other was finding a way to make a living and build a career that would allow me to thrive, not just survive. The job market was competitive, and I faced additional hurdles as a foreigner. Many employers preferred candidates with German qualifications, German experience, and a level of fluency that I had yet to achieve. I knew that finding a job in my field would be challenging, but I was determined not to settle, not to let go of the dreams that had brought me here.

I spent hours researching, applying for jobs, and crafting resumes highlighting my skills and experience. I would walk through the city, visit companies, introduce myself, and leave my resume wherever possible. Each rejection, each unanswered application, felt like a setback, but it also gave a leg-up to my determination. I reminded myself that every "no" brought me closer to a "yes" and that each door that closed was one less obstacle on the path to success. My hustle became a daily ritual, a routine of persistence that kept me focused and reminded me of the purpose that had brought me to this land.

Eventually, I found work, though it wasn't in my field. It was a temporary position, a role that didn't fully utilize my skills, but it was a start. I embraced it with gratitude, seeing it as an opportunity to learn, build connections, and gain experience within the German system. Each day on the job was a lesson in resilience, a reminder that success would not come quickly but that it was within reach. I showed up early, worked hard, and learned as much as possible. I was determined to prove myself, not only to my employers but to myself, to show that I could succeed, adapt, and thrive.

As I settled into my routine, I began to see progress, small but significant. My German improved; I could understand conversations more clearly and respond more confidently. My job, though modest, provided a sense of stability, a foundation upon which I could build. I started making friends, connecting with colleagues, and finding a sense of belonging within a community that had once felt foreign. Each day was a step forward, a testament to my resilience, and a reminder that determination could turn even the most minor victories into milestones.

Yet, the journey was far from easy. There were days when the weight of it all felt overwhelming, the struggles seemed too great, and the setbacks made me question my choices. On those days, I would remind myself why I had come here, the dreams that had carried me across borders, and the hopes that had driven me to leave behind everything I knew. I would think of my family, the sacrifices they had made, and the pride they felt in my journey. I would remind myself that each struggle and challenge was a step closer to the life I had envisioned and the success I was determined to achieve.

As I adjusted, I began to see Germany in a new light. The same structures that once felt restrictive now provided a sense of order, a foundation I could build. The discipline, precision, and routines became tools that I could use, qualities that I could incorporate into my life. I learned to value punctuality, appreciate German society's quiet efficiency, and find comfort in the predictability that had once felt so foreign. In a way, I was reshaping myself, blending my identity with the values of the society I was determined to be part of.

My hustle extended beyond work. I sought opportunities for personal growth, expanding my network, and connecting with others who shared my experiences. I joined community groups, attended events, and volunteered when I could. Each interaction, each connection, was a reminder that resilience was not just about surviving but about thriving, about finding joy and purpose even in the face of adversity. I discovered a community of other immigrants, people from all walks of life, each with their own story, struggles, and dreams. Together, we formed a support network, a reminder that, despite our differences, we were determined to succeed.

Through this network, I met mentors who guided me and helped me navigate the complexities of German society. They taught me about the unspoken rules, the nuances of social interactions, and the expectations that defined success in this new land. Their advice and support became a lifeline, a source of strength that helped me find my footing. I learned that resilience was not just about pushing forward alone but about leaning on others and building relationships that could sustain me in moments of doubt.

Over time, I began to see the fruits of my efforts. My language skills improved, my network expanded, and my career started to take shape. I found a job that aligned with my skills, a position that allowed me to grow, to contribute, to feel a sense of purpose. My hard work, determination, and resilience led me to a place where I could finally see a future, a life that felt both stable and fulfilling. The struggles had not disappeared, but I had learned to navigate them, to find strength within myself, and to keep moving forward even when the path was unclear.

Looking back, I realized the journey was as important as the destination. The struggles, setbacks, and moments of doubt shaped me, strengthened me, and taught me lessons I would carry with me for the rest of my life. Determination had become more than just a word; it was the force that had taken me through, the resilience that had allowed me to adapt, hustle, and find my footing in a land that had once felt foreign. Each challenge had been a step forward, each success a reminder of what I could achieve.

In Germany, I had found a place to live and grow and build a life of purpose and meaning. My journey had been one of transformation, of resilience, of determination. And as I looked toward the future, I knew I was ready for whatever lay ahead. The struggles had given me strength, the surprises had taught me resilience, and the determination that had carried me this far would continue to guide me as I carved out my path in this land of opportunity.

Chapter 3
The Systemic Web

GERMANY'S BUREAUCRACY is both a marvel and a mystery. To many, it represents the backbone of a society that values order, precision, and adherence to rules. The system appears seamless on paper, a carefully woven web designed to maintain stability and predictability in daily life. However, the bureaucratic system can feel like an impenetrable maze for foreigners, a series of tests and obstacles that seem almost purposefully complex. Each step forward is accompanied by a mountain of paperwork, an array of rules, and countless appointments, each feeling like navigating a web with no apparent way out.

My first experience with the German bureaucracy was registering my address, which was required for every resident, whether foreign or not. What seemed like a straightforward process quickly revealed the rigidity of the system. Armed with a rental agreement and identification, I arrived at the local registration office only to be met with endless people waiting. Each person held tightly onto their documents, their expressions a mix of determination and resignation. The line moved slowly, each appointment taking longer than expected as if the very structure of the office was designed to test one's patience.

Finally, my turn arrived, and I approached the counter with relief, only to discover that I was missing a single form—a tenant confirmation document signed by my landlord. The clerk's expression was blank, almost as if she had encountered this same mistake countless times. With a curt nod, she told me to return once I had the necessary paperwork. The entire process would have to start over. I left the office frustrated, aware that even the tiniest oversight could derail the process, that each requirement was non-negotiable, and that the system had no room for error.

This was only the beginning. Registering my address was the first in a series of bureaucratic hoops that marked the path to building a life in Germany. Every aspect of life requires a set of documents, each process's protocol. Opening a bank account, obtaining health insurance, applying for a work permit—each step demanded paperwork, appointments, and an understanding of a system that often felt intentionally complicated. This might have been second nature, a familiar part of life for locals. But for a foreigner, each encounter with bureaucracy was like venturing into unknown territory, a maze with ever-changing rules and requirements.

The most challenging part of the system was its inflexibility. Every document had to be precisely filled, every form correctly submitted, and every requirement meticulously met. There was no room for improvisation no flexibility in interpretation. The language barrier only compounded the difficulty. The forms were written in technical German and filled with terms and jargon I struggled to understand. I found myself translating every line, trying to decipher the meaning, hoping I hadn't missed a critical detail. A single mistake could mean starting over, and each delay felt like a setback on my journey to stability.

The bureaucratic system felt like an insurmountable barrier for foreigners trying to establish financial stability or start a business. Opening a business was my dream, a vision of independence and success that had driven me to Germany. But the process was overwhelming, with rules and regulations designed to deter anyone without intimate knowledge of the system. I needed permits, licenses, and approvals, each requiring its own set of documents, each step demanding yet another trip to an office, another appointment, another encounter with the rigid structure of German bureaucracy.

One of the most frustrating aspects of the system was the reliance on specific documents that seemed impossible to obtain as a newcomer. Many processes required proof of residency, German credit history, or references from previous employers in Germany. These requirements were simple for locals, who had grown up within the system, but for foreigners, they were a near-impossible hurdle. I was caught in a cycle of needing documents to obtain other documents, each step contingent on the previous one. It was as if the system was designed to keep foreigners on the periphery, to prevent us from fully integrating, from truly establishing ourselves within the framework of German society.

Financial stability was another challenge. Opening a bank account, for example, required proof of address, proof of income, and, in some cases, a German credit history. Without these, even the most basic financial tasks—paying rent, receiving a salary, managing expenses—became challenging. Many banks viewed foreigners as high-risk clients, often refusing services or demanding higher fees. I remember feeling frustrated as I explained my situation, only to be met with polite indifference. The rules were non-negotiable, and I was left to navigate a system that seemed intent on keeping me at arm's length.

The process of obtaining health insurance was equally daunting. Health insurance is mandatory in Germany for anyone wanting to work, study, or live there. However, finding affordable coverage was a challenge for foreigners, especially those without permanent contracts. The options were limited, accompanied by fine print pages, conditions, and exclusions. Private insurance came with high premiums, while public insurance required proof of employment, a catch-22 for those still trying to establish themselves. I spent countless hours researching, meeting with insurance agents, and trying to find a solution that would meet the requirements without breaking the bank. Each conversation, each document, was a reminder of the system's complexity, a maze that demanded patience and resilience.

The raw truth about the bureaucratic system in Germany is that it is not designed for newcomers. It is a structure built to serve those who understand its intricacies and those who have grown up within its confines. For foreigners, each encounter is a reminder of our outsider status, a test of our ability to adapt to navigate a system that feels both foreign and unforgiving. There were times when I felt defeated, when the sheer weight of the paperwork, the appointments, and the unyielding rules felt overwhelming. However, each setback only strengthened my determination, and each challenge reminded me of the resilience required to succeed.

There was a particular moment that encapsulated my experience with the German bureaucratic system—a moment that highlighted both the rigidity of the structure and the resilience it demanded. I had finally gathered all the documents needed to open a business account, a critical step in my journey toward establishing myself financially. I arrived at the bank, prepared confident, only to be told that one of my documents, a residency permit, had expired the day before. It was a minor detail, a single day's difference, but to the clerk behind the desk, it was enough to deny my application. I pleaded my case, explaining the oversight, but the rules were clear. I would have to renew the permit and start the process over again.

Leaving the bank that day, I felt a wave of frustration, a sense of helplessness that was infuriating and humbling. The system had no room for errors and no allowance for the unexpected. Each rule and regulation was an unyielding barrier, a reminder that my journey to financial stability and independence was far from straightforward. But even in that moment of defeat, I felt a renewed determination, a resolve to keep pushing forward, to find a way through the German bureaucratic system maze.

In time, I began understanding the rules and finding ways to work within the structure rather than against it. I learned to double-check every document, prepare for each appointment with meticulous detail, and approach each step with patience and resilience. I built connections, sought advice from others who had navigated the system, and found mentors who guided me through the complexities. Slowly, I began to see progress, to feel a sense of stability, a foundation upon which I could build.

Looking back, I realized that the bureaucratic system, as challenging as it was, had taught me invaluable lessons. It forced me to become resourceful, to approach each obstacle with a sense of purpose, and to develop a resilience that would carry me through future challenges. Though frustrating and often overwhelming, the maze of bureaucracy had shaped me, strengthened me, and prepared me for the journey ahead. While the web of rules and regulations remained, I had learned to navigate it, find my way through the complexities, and build a life in a country that both welcomed me and held me at a distance.

In Germany, success is not freely given; it is earned through persistence, an ability to adapt, and navigating a system that values order over flexibility. With all its rules and regulations, the bureaucratic web is a test of one's determination and resilience. As I looked toward the future, I knew the lessons I had learned and the challenges I had overcome would serve me well on the journey ahead. The systemic web was both a barrier and a teacher, a reminder that success in Germany required ambition and an unwavering resolve to keep pushing forward, find a way through the maze, and build a life of purpose and stability within a system that demanded nothing less.

Economic Hurdles

In Germany, the economy is a source of national pride, a machine that runs on precision, stability, and carefully crafted systems. The country is known for its strong job market, its robust financial institutions, and the sense of security that these systems provide. Yet, as a foreigner, I quickly discovered the hidden barriers within this system. Despite the promise of opportunity, the path to financial stability felt like an uphill battle designed to support locals at every turn. Job applications, housing, and loans were accompanied by obstacles invisible to locals but glaringly apparent to anyone trying to build a life from the outside.

The Job Market Maze

One of the first and most daunting economic hurdles was the job market. Germany's economy is renowned for its demand for skilled industrious, particularly in fields like engineering, technology, and healthcare. Yet, despite this demand, foreigners often find themselves sidelined, struggling to gain recognition for their qualifications and experience. For many, like myself, the reality of finding work that matched our skills and aspirations felt like an elusive goal. I held qualifications and experience that I knew were valuable, yet the German job market was a maze of requirements and unspoken preferences that seemed to prioritize local candidates.

One of the first barriers was the language. While many Germans speak English, fluency is often required for higher-level positions, even in fields where English might be the primary working language. Job descriptions would list "fluent German" as a requirement, immediately eliminating candidates who hadn't mastered the language. For a foreigner, job opportunities were limited initially, with many positions closed off simply due to language barriers. The paradox was apparent: Germany wanted skilled workers but made it nearly impossible for those same workers to qualify without advanced German language skills.

Beyond language, there was a preference for German qualifications. Many companies, particularly in traditional industries, preferred candidates with German degrees or certifications, often disregarding foreign qualifications regardless of their relevance or equivalency. I remember applying for positions where my experience matched the requirements perfectly, only to be told that my foreign degree was "unfamiliar" or "difficult to verify." In some cases, employers would suggest that I obtain additional German qualifications, a time-consuming and costly process that felt like an unnecessary barrier. These qualifications were given to locals who grew up in the German education system. However, for foreigners, they were yet another hurdle, a requirement designed to exclude rather than include.

Job applications themselves were often a process that highlighted the subtle preference for locals. In Germany, applications require more detail beyond the standard resume and cover letter. Employers expect a Lebenslauf (CV) that includes work experience and a photo, date of birth, and marital status—details that, in many countries, would be considered irrelevant or even discriminatory. For a foreigner, understanding and meeting these expectations was a challenge, a reminder that even the application process was tailored to those who understood the nuances of German professional culture.

Even once I secured a job, the challenges persisted. As a foreigner, I often felt that I was held to a different standard, that my work was scrutinized more closely, and that my mistakes were less easily forgiven. In some cases, colleagues and supervisors would hesitate to involve me in projects that required client interaction or public presentations, fearing that my "foreignness" might reflect poorly on the company. It was a subtle form of exclusion, a reminder that I was still seen as an outsider despite my qualifications and efforts.

The Housing Paradox

Finding stable housing was another economic hurdle that seemed to be designed for the locals citizens in any means. Germany's housing market is competitive, with high demand and limited supply, particularly in major cities. For foreigners, this competition is compounded by a set of requirements that are difficult to meet without an established presence in the country. Landlords typically require extensive documentation—proof of income, a German credit score, references from previous landlords, and sometimes even a German guarantor. For a newcomer, meeting these criteria was nearly impossible, creating a paradox where I needed stable housing to establish myself but couldn't secure housing without already being established.

One of the most challenging requirements was the SCHUFA, Germany's credit scoring system. SCHUFA reports are a standard requirement for most rental applications, providing landlords with a tenant's credit history and financial reliability. However, as a foreigner, I had no SCHUFA score or financial history in Germany. Without it, many landlords viewed me as a high-risk tenant, regardless of my ability to pay rent. I would present my employment contract, bank statements, and references from my home country, but without a SCHUFA score, these efforts often fell short.

This lack of credit history created a frustrating cycle. I needed stable housing to build a financial record, yet my lack of a financial record prevented me from securing stable housing. I would apply for apartment after apartment, only to be met with polite rejections or demands for documentation I didn't have. In some cases, landlords would offer me apartments at a higher rent or with additional security deposits, effectively penalizing me for my foreign status. Like the job market, the housing market felt like a system designed to enrich locals, with foreigners left to navigate a landscape of temporary rentals and sublets.

Loans and Financial Stability

Loans, whether for a car, a home, or a business, are often seen as a pathway to financial stability and growth. In Germany, however, the lending system is built on a foundation of trust that is difficult for foreigners to access. Banks rely heavily on SCHUFA scores and German credit histories to determine eligibility for loans, making it nearly impossible for newcomers to secure financing without years of financial history in the country.

When I first attempted to apply for a small loan, I was met with immediate unavoidable controversy. Despite having a steady income, my lack of credit history in Germany was viewed as a significant risk. The loan officer explained that the bank couldn't approve my application without a SCHUFA score and a record of my financial reliability within Germany. I offered to provide bank statements, proof of income, and even letters of recommendation, but these were dismissed as insufficient. The rules were clear: loans were out of reach without a German credit history and a SCHUFA score.

This restriction extended to other forms of financing as well. Leasing a car, applying for a credit card, and even signing up for certain utilities often required a credit check, one that I couldn't pass as a newcomer. It was as if the financial system was designed to exclude anyone without a pre-existing record within Germany, a system that implanted for those who had grown up within its confines. For a foreigner, this lack of access to credit was a significant barrier to financial stability, a reminder that, despite my efforts, I was still seen as a financial risk.

The restrictions on loans and credit also impacted my ability to pursue entrepreneurial opportunities. Starting a business had been one of my long-term goals, a vision of financial independence that had driven me to Germany. But this dream felt increasingly out of reach without access to financing or the ability to secure even a small loan.

The financial institutions were transparent in their requirements, and each rejection reminded me that the system was not designed for people like me.

Economic Disparities and Subtle Exclusions

Throughout these experiences, a pattern emerged—one of subtle exclusion, of barriers invisible to locals but all too visible to foreigners. With its rules and requirements, the economic system set-up for those who understood its intricacies and those who had grown up within its structure. For foreigners, each step was accompanied by an additional layer of complexity, a reminder that, despite the promise of opportunity, the path was anything but straightforward.

This exclusion extended to social interactions as well. In Germany, networking is crucial to career advancement, building connections, and finding opportunities. But as a foreigner, I often found myself outside these networks, struggling to break into a world that valued familiarity and trust. Colleagues would bond over shared experiences, language, and culture, creating a sense of belonging that felt just out of reach. In some cases, networking events and professional associations would conduct meetings exclusively in German, making it difficult for those still learning the language to participate fully. This linguistic barrier and cultural differences created a sense of isolation, a reminder that, despite my efforts, I was still navigating a system that opened doors beyond insiders.

The raw reality of these economic hurdles is that they are not always overtly discriminatory; they are embedded within the structures of a system that values stability and predictability. Each requirement, each document, and each credit check is part of a larger framework designed to protect the economy and maintain a sense of order.

However, for foreigners, this framework can feel like a fortress, a series of walls that prevent full participation in the country's financial life.

Looking back, I realize that these frustrating hurdles also taught me valuable lessons about resilience and adaptability. They forced me to find alternative paths to approach each obstacle creatively and determinedly. I learned to rely on personal savings, gradually build my credit history, and seek out landlords willing to take a chance on a foreign tenant. Each success, each small victory, was hard-earned, a testament to the strength required to navigate a system that, by design, luxury locals.

Resilience and Resourcefulness

Navigating Germany's economic landscape as a foreigner was akin to climbing a steep mountain, with each step revealing new challenges designed to test one's determination. For someone unfamiliar with the system's intricacies, every setback was a reminder of the economic paradoxes embedded within the structure of German society. Despite its reputation as a land of opportunity, the hurdles foreigners face often highlight the balance between stability and exclusion. But with each challenge, I grew more resourceful, learning to adapt and develop strategies that allowed me to navigate this structured environment in unconventional ways. Each rejection, each delay, and each roadblock engendered determination to make the system work for me, even if it meant approaching the journey with creativity and resilience.

Confronting Financial Exclusion and Developing Workarounds

One of the first challenges was securing financial resources without a German credit history. Banks and financial institutions here operate on a system of trust built over time, and for a foreigner with no established credit, this presented a considerable barrier. But rather than allowing the lack of access to loans to hinder my progress, I developed a new approach: building credit on my terms. I established a record of reliable financial stable through small, consistent transactions with local banks. This involved setting up a modest savings account, ensuring I made regular deposits, and demonstrating financial responsibility through disciplined budgeting.

Eventually, I found a smaller, more flexible bank willing to work with foreigners. I leveraged my employment contract and steady income as proof of reliability, gradually earning a form of financial trust. While these smaller banks came with higher fees and stricter conditions, they offered an entry point that allowed me to build a financial history within the system. Over time, this opened avenues for accessing limited credit options, allowing me to move forward with more excellent stability.

Overcoming Housing Discrimination with a Network-Based Strategy

Housing was another area where traditional methods often fell short. Without a German credit history, finding long-term housing was challenging. I realized that conventional methods, like applying directly through rental agencies, usually led to rejections, but networking and direct recommendations held more weight. I connected with people within the foreign community who had been in Germany for longer, tapping into their networks and learning about landlords more open to renting to foreigners.

One approach I developed was to attend community events and build relationships within these networks. Through social connections, I could gather referrals from people familiar with newcomers' struggles. This network-based strategy allowed me to find housing opportunities that were otherwise inaccessible through traditional channels. In many cases, simply having a reference from someone trusted by the landlord was enough to bypass some of the strict requirements typically expected of newcomers.

Employment: Navigating a Different Standard with an Entrepreneurial Mindset

Securing meaningful employment as a foreigner in Germany was perhaps one of my most complex challenges. The standards for hiring, particularly in roles that required client-facing interactions, were often shaped by unspoken expectations. While I faced instances where language and cultural biases hindered my job prospects, I began to rethink how I could present my skills in a way that made me valuable to potential employers.

I crafted a unique personal brand, emphasizing my international experience as an asset rather than a liability. Instead of conforming to traditional resumes, I designed a portfolio that highlighted the diversity of my skills and the unique perspective I brought to the table. By positioning myself as someone who could offer insights into global markets and bring creative problem-solving to culturally diverse teams, I found that some employers began to see me as a bridge between local and international perspectives. Over time, this approach helped me secure roles that valued my expertise and respected the adaptability and resilience I had developed.

For employers who were hesitant about my foreign background, I created a proposal system where I outlined specific projects or tasks I could complete, allowing them to "test" my skills on a contract basis. This approach allowed me to build a track record and establish professional credibility within German companies that might have initially hesitated to hire a foreigner for permanent roles. It required patience and flexibility, but it was a strategy that ultimately allowed me to gain experience within my field and build a professional reputation.

Developing Resourceful Solutions for Bureaucratic Challenges

Germany's bureaucratic system, with its myriad rules and documentation requirements, often felt impenetrable. But with each setback, I became more adept at navigating this maze, crafting strategies to overcome bureaucratic obstacles with minimal disruption. One effective method I developed was to prepare for each appointment, double-check each document meticulously, ensure I had everything required, and even bring additional documentation in case of unexpected requirements. I learned to anticipate potential issues by researching other foreigners' experiences and adapting my approach based on their challenges.

To handle the language barrier in bureaucratic settings, I created a personal glossary of standard bureaucratic terms and phrases in German, allowing me to understand documents and fill out forms accurately. I also reached out to volunteer translation services and local organizations that offered support to foreigners navigating bureaucracy. Over time, I developed a system of personal "templates" for everyday bureaucratic tasks, allowing me to prepare more efficiently for future processes.

When issues arose, I also learned the value of persistence. Returning to the same office multiple times, even if it meant waiting in line or requesting assistance from a different clerk, often led to more opportunity outcomes. By being persistent and showing my commitment to fulfilling the requirements, I found that some bureaucrats were more willing to work with me. In a system that values order, demonstrating a willingness to follow procedures, even at the expense of personal time, sometimes garnered a degree of respect and flexibility that I hadn't anticipated.

Resourcefulness in Overcoming Financial Constraints

Without immediate access to traditional credit options, I had to get creative in managing my finances and planning for long-term goals. One strategy I developed was to leverage international financial resources, such as using credit cards from my home country with beneficial international terms. This allowed me to maintain a line of credit while building my financial profile in Germany. I also focused on building personal savings, adopting a strict budgeting system that accounted for both immediate needs and long-term goals. I learned to prioritize essential expenses and identify opportunities for saving, allowing me to gradually accumulate financial stability without relying on loans.

Additionally, I researched alternative financing options, such as microloans and small business grants available to foreigners and new entrepreneurs. While these options were limited, they provided a stepping stone that allowed me to pursue business ideas without the burden of traditional debt. This approach required resilience and resourcefulness, but it was an essential part of navigating the economic constraints of the system.

Chapter 3
Hustling in the Shadows

GERMANY IS KNOWN FOR its structured, formal economy—where work, business, and finance follow strict rules and regulations. But beneath this well-ordered exterior lies a world where foreign entrepreneurs, freelancers, and hustlers operate within a parallel economy. This "shadow economy" isn't necessarily illegal. Still, it exists outside the traditional frameworks, where foreigners find alternative ways to make a living and create opportunities in an environment that isn't always welcoming. These underground networks are built on the resilience of those excluded from the mainstream economy, offering a lifeline to those willing to hustle, adapt, and find a way forward despite the obstacles.

When I first encountered this world, I was taken aback by its vibrancy and resourcefulness. These were people from all walks of life—immigrants, refugees, international students, and expatriates—each with a story of why they had come to Germany and how they were trying to make it. For many, the formal economy had proven too difficult to break into due to language barriers, strict job requirements, or lack of recognition for foreign qualifications. They were skilled, ambitious, and determined, but the system's constraints had left them on the sidelines. In response, they had created their own spaces, opportunities, and economy, operating in what could be described as the shadows of Germany's economic landscape.

The Diverse World of Side-Gigs and Informal Work

One of the most common forms of hustle in these underground networks was through side gigs and informal work. In major cities like Berlin, Hamburg, and Munich, you can find foreign workers offering services that range from catering and cleaning to graphic design and translation. Many of these individuals were highly skilled professionals—engineers, teachers, artists—who had been unable to find work in their fields due to the barriers in the formal job market. Instead, they offered their skills directly to the community, building a client base through word of mouth, online platforms, and informal networks.

Cafés and restaurants became networking hubs where people could exchange contact information and discuss potential gigs. Unofficial "job boards" were posted on walls in immigrant-owned businesses, offering everything from weekend painting jobs to freelance photography gigs. These weren't high-paying opportunities, but they provided a way for people to make a living, survive, and, in some cases, thrive. The beauty of this underground economy was its flexibility and ability to adapt to the community's needs. Unlike the rigid structures of the formal economy, these networks operated on trust, reputation, and the shared understanding that everyone was trying to find their place.

Entrepreneurs in the Shadows: Building Businesses from Scratch

For those with a more entrepreneurial spirit, the shadow economy offered a platform to start small businesses. These ventures were often launched with limited resources, using personal savings or support from friends and family. Immigrant-owned shops, food stalls, and market stands became popular among the foreign community, offering products and services that reminded them of home while catering to the broader community's interest in diversity and multiculturalism.

Take, for example, the story of Ahmed, a Syrian refugee who arrived in Germany with little more than a dream and a strong work ethic. Back home, he had been a chef known for his family's traditional recipes. Ahmed could not find work in local restaurants due to language barriers and the strict certification requirements in the German culinary industry, so he decided to start his small food stall at local markets. He sold falafel, shawarma, and other Middle Eastern dishes, initially relying on his community's support but gradually expanding to a broader clientele. The local market space allowed him to work informally, bypassing the requirements of a formal restaurant while building his reputation as a skilled chef. Over time, he became well-known in his Area, and his business grew, proving that there was room for entrepreneurship even in the shadows.

These entrepreneurial ventures were not without their challenges. Navigating the legal requirement was a constant struggle. Many immigrants lacked the financial resources to hire legal or business consultants, so they relied on advice from friends, online forums, and trial and error. Some businesses operated in a legal grey area, stretching the limits of what was permissible, while others worked entirely informally. For example, pop-up restaurants, catering services from home kitchens, and informal childcare were standard. These businesses often operated under the radar, providing vital services within the community but vulnerable to shutdowns if authorities took notice.

Community Solidarity and Informal Networks

One of the most remarkable aspects of this shadow economy was the solidarity among its participants. Foreigners from different backgrounds came together, sharing resources, knowledge, and support. There was an understanding that, while everyone came from other places and faced unique challenges, they were all navigating the same complex system, and there was strength in unity.

In these networks, skills were exchanged rather than purchased. A graphic designer might help a restaurant owner with marketing materials in exchange for meals, or a mechanic might fix a fellow immigrant's car for free, knowing that the favor would one day be returned. These informal arrangements were based on mutual respect and trust, filling gaps left by the formal economy and creating a resilient and adaptable support system.

Another powerful aspect of these networks was their sense of identity and community. In a society where many foreigners felt invisible or marginalized, these informal networks provided a sense of belonging. They offered a place to speak one's native language, to celebrate cultural traditions, and to share stories of resilience. It was in these networks that I heard stories of success, stories of failure, and stories of dreams that were still being pursued despite the odds. Each person contributed to the community by sharing their skills, providing emotional support, or offering practical advice on navigating Germany's complex systems.

The Risk and Reward of Operating in the Shadows

While the shadow economy offered opportunities, it also came with risks. Working informally meant that many hustlers and side gig workers lacked the protections provided by the formal economy. There was no social security, health insurance, or legal recourse in disputes. A missed payment or an exploitative client could have devastating consequences, and there was little they could do to seek justice. This vulnerability was a constant reminder of their situation's precariousness and the thin line they walked between survival and instability.

Despite these risks, many were willing to take the chance. The lack of alternatives and the sense of agency from working independently made the shadow economy an attractive option. People took pride in their work and their ability to provide for themselves and their families, even if it meant operating outside the boundaries of the formal economy. For many, the rewards outweighed the risks, and their resilience built through these experiences became a source of strength and pride.

One typical story was that of Maria, a Brazilian immigrant who provided cleaning services for private households. While her work was informal, she built a client base that valued her skills and reliability. Maria relied on referrals, building her reputation within her community and beyond. But she also faced risks: clients could refuse to pay, disputes over expectations were common, and without legal contracts, she had little recourse in such situations. Still, she continued, driven by her determination to build a life for herself and her family. Like many others in the shadow economy, her story reflected the resilience, adaptability, and resourcefulness required to succeed in a system that didn't always acknowledge their efforts.

Adapting and Thriving: Lessons Learned from the Shadow Economy

Operating within the shadows taught me invaluable lessons about adaptability, resilience, and the power of community. I learned that Germany's formal economy might be challenging to access, but the foreign community had created its pathways to success. These were people who had faced setbacks, rejection, and exclusion but who refused to give up. Instead, they had crafted an alternative economy, a network of support that defied the limitations imposed by the formal system.

The shadow economy also forced me to develop a new set of skills. I learned how to negotiate, market myself, navigate complex social dynamics, and build relationships based on trust and mutual benefit. These skills weren't taught in classrooms or formal workplaces but were essential for survival in the shadow economy. In this world, success is measured not only by financial gain but by one's ability to adapt, persevere, and find creative solutions in the face of adversity.

Looking back, I realize that the shadow economy was not merely a response to exclusion but a testament to the resilience of those who participated. This world of hustlers, entrepreneurs, and side gig workers was a reminder that opportunity exists even in the most challenging circumstances and that resilience can transform setbacks into success. While the shadow economy operates on the margins, it is a vibrant, dynamic force, a parallel economy that reflects the ingenuity and determination of those who refuse to be defined by the limitations imposed upon them.

Friendships and Rivalries

In Germany's shadow economy, friendships and rivalries form the fabric of a community where support and competition coexist in a delicate balance. For foreigners, building a life here often means creating alliances with those who understand the journey—fellow immigrants and expatriates who share the same obstacles, ambitions, and dreams. Yet, within this shared struggle, competition can be intense, as resources and opportunities are scarce. Friendships offer strength, advice, and solidarity, while rivalries can bring out fierce competition, where every contact, client, or job becomes a prized asset. These relationships create a complex web of camaraderie and contention, a network where people lift each other and vie for limited success.

The Formation of Alliances

One of the first friendships I formed was with Eduardo, a Brazilian who had come to Germany around the same time as I did. Eduardo was a handyman by trade, skilled in plumbing, electrical work, and carpentry. Like me, he had struggled to find work in his field within the formal economy, so he turned to freelance gigs he could pick up within our community. Eduardo and I met at a networking event for foreigners, and a shared frustration with Germany's bureaucratic and economic hurdles, traumatised our initial connection. We quickly discovered that we could help each other—while I had more formal experience with specific clients, Eduardo had a strong work ethic and practical skills that allowed him to excel in hands-on projects.

Together, we devised a system to exchange skills. He would assist me with more practical, intensive jobs, while I would help him with paperwork, crafting marketing materials, and securing new clients. Eduardo introduced me to several clients needing services I could provide, and I did the same for him. Our friendship was rooted in this mutual benefit, but it was also more profound than just a professional exchange. Eduardo understood my struggles and encouraged me on days when everything felt insurmountable. We shared advice, tips, and laughs, lifting each other as we tried to succeed in an environment that didn't facilitate foreigners.

Our alliance, however, was not without its occasional tension. As we grew more skilled and confident, the line between cooperation and competition began to blur. We found ourselves vying for the same clients occasionally, each hoping to secure a project that would provide much-needed income. It was an unspoken rivalry, a quiet competition that never surfaced into confrontation, but it was there. We both understood that, as much as we supported each other, survival often came down to who could land the next client.

The Supportive Network: A Circle of Allies

Eduardo was not the only ally I found. The shadow economy was filled with foreigners who offered their services and support. Take Maria, a Filipina woman who had established herself as a highly sought-after cleaner for private households. Maria was resourceful and connected, quickly becoming essential to my network. Maria introduced me to clients, referred me to friends, and taught me the ins and outs of dealing with private households—a market with unspoken rules and expectations.

Maria's generosity was genuine, and her support significantly impacted my early days. She shared her strategies for building trust with clients, explained how to handle misunderstandings, and even taught me key German phrases that helped me navigate conversations more smoothly. Maria was a mentor, a friend, and a lifeline in a world that often felt isolating. Her support allowed me to access a circle of clients I might not have reached, and I was grateful for her kindness.

At the same time, there was an unspoken understanding that we were all in this for ourselves. Maria and I shared clients but also respected each other's boundaries. If she referred a client to me, I knew loyalty to her must be maintained; I would never attempt to take her clients away. The informal economy had its code of ethics, a set of rules we all followed to avoid stepping on each other's toes. Friendships were built on trust, but everyone knew that trust was delicate—breaking it could mean being cut off from crucial referrals and resources.

When Friendships Become Rivalries

In some cases, friendships didn't last. The shadow economy's competitive nature often strained relationships, turning allies into competitors as everyone scrambled for limited opportunities. One of the most striking examples of this transformation was my relationship with Carlos, a Spanish web designer with a knack for digital marketing. Carlos and I had initially bonded over our shared interest in entrepreneurship. We often exchanged clients, referred work to each other, and discussed ways to navigate the freelance market.

However, as our respective businesses grew, so did our competition. Clients sometimes contacted us for similar work, forcing us into direct competition. At first, it was subtle—we would try to secure the client by offering a slightly lower rate or promising a quicker turnaround time. But as demand increased, so did the stakes. We began seeing each other as competitors rather than collaborators, each vying for a market share that felt just out of reach.

Our rivalry came to a head when a high-paying client, whom we had both been courting for months, ultimately chose Carlos over me. I was disappointed but understood that this was part of the hustle. However, learning later that Carlos had subtly undercut me by promising the client exclusive services and faster delivery times stung. The experience left me feeling betrayed, and while we maintained a professional relationship, the trust we had shared was fractured. From then on, I viewed Carlos less as an ally and more as a competitor, someone who might support me when it suited him but would ultimately look out for his interests above all else.

The Delicate Balance: A Tightrope Between Support and Survival

Navigating friendships and rivalries in the shadow economy required a careful balance. Building relationships was essential to survival, yet the constant competition meant no friendship was immune to tension. Trust was a precious resource, carefully given and closely guarded. Among us, loyalty was respected, but only to a point. Everyone understood that we were all trying to survive, to carve out a piece of the economy for ourselves.

In some cases, this balance led to unexpected alliances. I remember working on a project with Fatima, a Moroccan woman who had been a seamstress before moving to Germany. Fatima was incredibly skilled with her hands and keen eye for design. She had built a small but loyal client base in the foreign community, offering tailoring services and creating custom clothing on demand. When we first met, we saw each other as potential rivals, each concerned that the other might take away clients. But as we got to know each other, we realized our skills complemented. I could help her with marketing, and she could teach me valuable skills related to garment repair and customization.

Over time, Fatima and I formed a partnership, referring clients to one another, splitting costs for shared resources, and even collaborating on projects. She became one of my closest allies, someone I could count on not only for professional support but for friendship as well. Finding someone like Fatima was a gift in the shadow economy, where trust was rare and competition fierce. Our friendship reminded me that, even in a world of scarcity, there was room for collaboration and that sometimes success could be shared rather than hoarded.

Navigating the Complex Web of Relationships

The shadow economy's unique blend of friendship and rivalry taught me valuable lessons about human nature, loyalty, and resilience. In this world, relationships were fluid, shifting between support and competition as circumstances changed. I learned to cultivate alliances carefully, to nurture friendships without expecting unwavering loyalty, and to approach rivalries with respect rather than resentment. It was a delicate move, a tightrope walked where every interaction required a delicate balance of trust and caution.

I also learned that competition was inevitable and didn't have to be destructive. Some rivals became my most outstanding teachers, pushing me to improve my skills, work harder, and refine my approach. They challenged me to rise to the occasion better, and in many ways, I grew because of the competition. There were days when the tension felt overwhelming when I questioned whether it was worth it, but the friendships I formed, the alliances I built, and the lessons I learned kept me moving forward.

The shadow economy was not easy to navigate, but a world of resilience, determination, and survival. It was where foreigners, marginalized by the formal economy, came together to create their path. Friendships offered strength and support, while rivalries sharpened our resolve. We were all hustling, each finding our way in the shadows, driven by the desire to succeed in a system that often left us behind. The friendships and rivalries we formed were not just relationships; they were the foundation upon which we built our lives, a testament to the resilience and resourcefulness required to thrive in a world of scarcity and competition.

Sacrifices

Success in Germany's shadow economy doesn't come without its costs. For every small victory, there were sacrifices—time, comfort, and even my pride—that I had to make along the way. When I first arrived, I had dreams of creating a stable, prosperous life, but the reality of achieving that was much harsher and more complex than I had anticipated. As each hurdle presented itself, I realized that pursuing this life would mean giving up parts of myself and my expectations, accepting moments of discomfort, and facing brutal truths. These sacrifices were painful and often humbling, yet they became part of the journey that forged my resilience and shaped my path forward.

The Relentless Toll of Time

The first and most enduring sacrifice was time. In Germany, where systems and rules guard stability, establishing oneself can be prolonged, particularly for a foreigner trying to break into the shadow economy. The time I could have spent with friends, on hobbies, or simply resting was consumed by work and the relentless pursuit of survival. Each day became a cycle of tasks that left little room for personal enjoyment or leisure. While others could plan their weekends or take breaks, I constantly hustled, seeking new clients, completing gigs, or preparing for the next day's work.

Building a reputation in the shadow economy was a time-intensive process. Every client interaction and job were an opportunity to establish trust and build my network. But it also meant long hours, often beyond what I had initially agreed upon, as clients would sometimes ask for "a little extra" or surprise me with additional tasks that needed completion. Saying no wasn't always an option—every client could be a potential source of future referrals, and rejecting their requests could mean lost opportunities. As a result, I often found myself working late into the night, missing out on rest, and sacrificing sleep to ensure I maintained my reputation.

The nature of freelance and informal work also meant no "steady schedule." Jobs could come in sporadically, and I had to be available whenever the opportunity presented itself. There were days when I worked from morning until well past midnight, juggling multiple gigs to make ends meet. Weekends, holidays, and evenings became just another workday, the line between personal time and work-life blurring until they became indistinguishable. Time, once something I could manage and control, became something I sacrificed continuously. I realized that building a life here meant accepting that the demands on my time would be constant and unrelenting.

Comfort: Living with the Bare Essentials

I sacrificed physical comfort as I dedicated more of my time to work. My resources were limited, and investing in luxuries or basic comforts felt impractical when every euro mattered. My living situation, for example, was far from ideal. In the early days, finding affordable housing was challenging, and the only option I could secure was a modest, cramped room in a shared apartment. The space was small, the furnishings were minimal, and privacy was a luxury I didn't have. My roommates were also hustlers, foreigners trying to make their way, and while we shared an understanding of each other's struggles, the lack of personal space made it hard to relax, unwind, or feel genuinely at home.

Simple comforts I had once taken for granted—like a clean, quiet living space or a warm, home-cooked meal—became rare. The hustle demanded that I prioritize work over everything else, including my living environment. My room became a place to sleep, not a home. There were nights when I would return from a long day, exhausted, only to find that my roommates were using the space for their side hustles, turning the small apartment into a makeshift office, studio, or workshop. Privacy was a sacrifice, something I gave up in pursuing stability.

Financial sacrifices extended to food and health as well. Eating out or buying fresh ingredients became a luxury, so I lived on cheap, convenient meals—instant noodles, canned foods, and anything that was filling but cost-effective. There were days when I'd skip meals, choosing to save my money for more urgent expenses. This lifestyle took a toll on my health, but seeing a doctor felt like a financial burden I couldn't afford. For minor illnesses or aches, I would rely on over-the-counter medicine or push through, hoping that rest would be enough to keep me going. Physical discomfort became a regular part of life, an acceptance of the reality that I couldn't afford the luxuries of good food, healthcare, or even consistent self-care.

The Humbling Sacrifice of Pride

Perhaps the most challenging sacrifice was pride. Entering the shadow economy meant taking on work often undervalued, overlooked, and sometimes even looked down upon. I took jobs I would never have considered back home, from cleaning homes to working in warehouses to odd jobs requiring manual Hard Work. It was humbling work, tasks that demanded physical effort and sometimes came with little recognition. There were moments when clients would treat me with indifference or even disrespect, viewing me not as a skilled worker but as an outsider providing a service. These interactions were painful, but I swallowed my pride and carried on, knowing that this work was a means to an end.

Accepting menial work was often necessary to pay the bills, and I found myself in situations that forced me to confront my expectations. As someone who had come to Germany hoping to build a successful career, taking on such jobs felt like a step backward. I struggled with feelings of inadequacy, realizing that I was no longer seen as the professional I had once been but rather as a foreign worker struggling to make a living. Yet, I knew that holding onto pride would only hinder my progress. I had to let go to embrace each job as a stepping stone, no matter how small or insignificant it seemed.

The hustle also required me to sacrifice personal pride when dealing with clients and competitors. I often had to negotiate, lower my rates, or agree to conditions I knew were unfair to secure work. There were moments when I felt exploited when clients would demand extra work without compensation, and I knew that I had no choice but to comply. Speaking out could mean losing my job or damaging my reputation, so I learned to stay silent and accept situations that compromised my dignity, all for the sake of survival.

Even within my community of fellow hustlers, there was a need to manage my pride carefully. Sharing my struggles, admitting my failures, and seeking help were all acts that required humility. In a network where competition was fierce, where everyone was trying to prove themselves, admitting weakness felt like a risk. Yet, to form alliances and gain support, I had to be honest about my struggles, let down my guard, and seek advice. I learned that pride was often an obstacle, a barrier that could isolate me if I didn't let it go. Each time I asked for help or shared a failure, I had to set aside my pride, understanding that humility was a sacrifice I needed to make to survive in this environment.

The Emotional Sacrifice: Isolation and Loneliness

One of the more subtle but profound sacrifices was the emotional toll of isolation and loneliness. The relentless hustle left little time for social interactions or friendships outside the other hustlers' immediate circle. I missed family and friends and the sense of connection from community involvement. But socializing felt like time wasted, an indulgence I couldn't afford. As a result, I often found myself alone, dealing with the weight of my struggles in silence.

The isolation extended beyond physical separation; it was a psychological distance from living in a world many people around me couldn't understand. The friends I made in the foreign community were supportive, but everyone focused on survival. We rarely had the opportunity to connect on a deeper level, as we were preoccupied with our challenges and hustle. Genuine friendships became rare, replaced by alliances built on mutual benefit and practicality. While these relationships were valuable, they lacked the warmth and trust of faithful companionship, leaving me emotionally detached.

Loneliness became a constant companion, a reminder of my sacrifices to pursue a better life. I knew this isolation was a choice, a consequence of prioritizing work over everything else, but it didn't make it any easier. The emotional strain of constantly striving, competing, and trying to survive in a foreign country without a robust support system weighed heavily on me. There were days when the burden felt overwhelming, and the sacrifices seemed too great, but I reminded myself of why I was here, of the dreams that had brought me to Germany.

Chapter 4
Shadows of Doubt

IN EVERY JOURNEY OF perseverance, there are moments when the weight of hardships grows unbearable, and even the strongest resolve begins to waver. For all my determination, there were times when setbacks became overwhelming, the obstacles I faced seemed impossible, and doubt crept in like a shadow. These moments tested my spirit, moments when my dreams felt distant and my efforts futile. In Germany, where stability is revered and rules are strictly upheld, every setback felt like a personal failure, and each challenge reminded me of how foreign I was in this structured land. No matter how determined I was, my economic hardships occasionally overshadowed my hope, filling me with doubt about my place, abilities, and future.

The Frustration of Financial Insecurity

The constant struggle for financial security was one of the first economic hardships that eroded my confidence. The shadow economy offered opportunities but was inconsistent, unreliable, and often paid below an affordable cost of living. No matter how many hours I worked or gigs I took, there was always a lingering uncertainty about whether I would have enough to cover my expenses. Rent, bills, food—each became a source of anxiety, a monthly reminder of the precariousness of my situation.

There were days when I would count every euro, sacrificing even the most minor comforts to make ends meet. It was a humbling experience that brought out a vulnerability I hadn't anticipated. I began to question whether I could build a stable life here, whether the sacrifices were worth it, or if I was chasing an unattainable dream. The constant financial strain weighed on me, and in my lowest moments, I would wonder if I was failing myself and the hopes and Dreams, I had carried with me.

The Job Rejections That Stung Deeply

Perhaps the most disheartening moments came from the job rejections that seemed to pile up despite my best efforts. I spent hours preparing applications, carefully tailoring each resume, and crafting cover letters highlighting my skills, experience, and dedication. Yet, more often than not, the responses were polite rejections, emails that thanked me for my interest but stated that I was "not the right fit." Sometimes, there was no response—a silent reminder that my efforts were unseen, unacknowledged, and unvalued.

Each rejection stung, a blow to my self-esteem that made me question my abilities. I knew I was capable and had valuable skills, but the constant rejections eroded my confidence. I started to wonder if there was something fundamentally wrong with me or if I lacked something essential that employers in Germany were looking for. The doubt became a whisper that lingered in the back of my mind, a reminder of the countless doors that had closed on me. The rejection letters weren't just setbacks—they were symbols of a system that seemed unwilling to let me in, barriers that made me feel like I would never belong.

The most challenging part was knowing that much of this rejection was beyond my control. The preference for German qualifications, the requirement for fluent German, and the cultural expectations all disadvantaged me. No matter how hard I worked to improve my skills, there was always a sense that I was competing on uneven ground and that my efforts would never be enough to overcome the limitations imposed by my foreign background. This feeling of powerlessness was one of the most overwhelming aspects of my journey, a shadow that darkened even my most determined moments.

Questioning My Choices

As the economic hardships mounted, there were times when I found myself questioning the choices that had brought me to Germany in the first place. I had come here with dreams of building a better life and creating stability and success in a country known for its prosperity. Yet, the reality I faced was far from what I had envisioned. I had left behind family, friends, a familiar language, and a culture that embraced me. In exchange, I had found myself where every step forward seemed to require twice the effort, where even the most superficial achievements felt monumental.

I wondered if I had been naïve if I had romanticized the idea of life in Germany without fully understanding the challenges I would face. Was I chasing an illusion? Had I made a mistake in leaving behind everything I knew for a country that seemed indifferent to my struggles? These questions haunted me in my quietest moments, filling me with doubt and regret. It was painful to consider that the dreams I had held onto so tightly might have been misguided and that my hopes for a better life might never materialize as I had imagined.

There were nights when I would lie awake, replaying my decisions, wondering if a different path or choice might have spared me from these hardships. The doubt was hindered, a shadow that made even the idea of hope feel distant. I felt as though I were trapped between two worlds—the life I had left behind and the life I was trying to build, neither of which felt fully within my grasp.

Isolation and the Weight of Loneliness

Economic hardships are not just about money—they also bring a sense of isolation and loneliness that can be just as overwhelming. In Germany, where the culture values privacy and personal boundaries, finding the emotional support and camaraderie I had known back home was difficult. I missed the warmth of my family, the comfort of friends who understood me without explanation, and the sense of belonging from being in a familiar place. Here, every connection felt transactional, every relationship tinged with a sense of distance.

My economic struggles only amplified this loneliness. The need to constantly work, hustle, and secure the next gig or client left little time for socializing or building meaningful relationships. And even when I did meet people, there was always a barrier—a language barrier, a cultural barrier, or simply the fact that my struggles were not something they could fully understand. The shadow of doubt grew darker in these moments of isolation, filling me with a sense of detachment from the world around me. I felt like I was drifting, disconnected from the life I had hoped to build.

In my lowest moments, I would question whether I even belonged in Germany or could integrate into a society that often felt closed off. The loneliness reminded me of my outsider status, a feeling that no matter how hard I tried, I would never indeed be part of this place. This sense of not belonging was one of the most painful aspects of my journey, a shadow that followed me through every struggle and every setback, whispering that perhaps I was destined to remain on the margins.

Doubt in My Abilities and Worth

Economic hardships can chip away at one's sense of self-worth. As I faced setback after setback, I began to doubt my abilities, to question whether I was truly capable of achieving the life I had envisioned. The constant struggle to secure work, the rejection from job applications, and the difficulty in finding stable housing—all of these experiences made me feel as though I were failing as a professional and a person.

I started to internalize these setbacks, believing that perhaps I was lacking and not good enough. The shadow of doubt became a constant presence, a voice that reminded me of every rejection, every missed opportunity, every mistake. I would compare my progress to that of others, wondering why success seemed so much easier for them while I struggled with even the most minor steps. This comparison only deepened my doubt, reinforcing the belief that I was falling short and that my efforts would never be enough.

Even when I achieved small victories, the doubt lingered. I would question whether these successes were deserved, whether I had truly earned them or stumbled upon them by chance. This self-doubt became a barrier to my progress, a shadow that dimmed the light of hope even in moments of triumph. It was a constant reminder of the fragility of my confidence, the sense that my achievements were temporary, that the next setback was just around the corner.

Resilience in the Face of Doubt

Despite the shadows of doubt, a part of me refused to give up. Every setback, every moment of self-doubt, was a test of my resilience, a challenge to my determination. I reminded myself that I had come this far, had already overcome so much and that giving up now would mean abandoning everything I had worked for. The doubt was confirmed, and the hardships were overwhelming, but so was my resolve to keep going and find a way forward despite the obstacles.

In these moments of doubt, I found strength in remembering my purpose and reminding myself of the dreams that had brought me here. I thought of the life I wanted to build, the stability I sought, the sense of accomplishment I craved. These dreams became my anchor, a source of motivation that kept me moving even when everything felt impossible.

The shadows of doubt reminded me of the hardships that defined my journey. But I knew these shadows could only hold me back if I allowed them to. I chose to see each setback as a lesson, each moment of doubt as an opportunity to grow, strengthen my resolve and prove to myself that I could achieve my goals. The journey was difficult, and the sacrifices were great, but I was determined to keep moving forward.

The Psychological Impact of Uncertainty and Isolation

Moving to Germany was meant to begin a new chapter, a chance to build a life filled with stability, security, and success. However, as the economic challenges mounted and the sense of not fully belonging became more pervasive, the psychological toll became harder to ignore. Each setback, each rejection, and each moment of exclusion had a cumulative effect, chipping away at my confidence, my self-worth, and even my sense of identity. While I had expected challenges, I hadn't anticipated the profound emotional weight of constantly struggling in a place full of opportunity and impenetrably closed off. The psychological impact of these experiences was profound and complex, shaping not only my daily life but also my understanding of myself and my place in the world.

The Weight of Constant Uncertainty

One of the most profound effects of navigating Germany's shadow economy was the overwhelming uncertainty that colored every aspect of my life. Unlike those with stable jobs or secure housing, my future felt unpredictable, as though it could unravel any moment. No matter how hard I worked, the lack of a safety net and the precarious nature of my work meant that every month was a gamble. I often wondered if I would have enough to cover the rent if my next client fell through or if I could find new opportunities in time to make ends meet. The weight of this uncertainty was a constant, unyielding pressure that settled in my chest like a stone, a daily reminder that I was never truly secure.

The impact of this uncertainty extended beyond finances; it began to infiltrate my thoughts, emotions, and even identity. I became hyper-aware of every potential setback, every possible scenario that could destabilize the delicate balance I was trying to maintain. This constant state of vigilance, of bracing for the next crisis, drained me emotionally. I found it hard to relax, feel at ease, and enjoy even the most minor pleasures because my mind was always racing, calculating, and preparing for the worst.

This sense of perpetual instability left me feeling powerless, as though I had no control over my life. No matter how meticulously I planned or how hard I worked, there was always a lingering fear that something could go wrong—a client might cancel, a job opportunity might vanish, or a bureaucratic hurdle could arise. The uncertainty gnawed at my sense of security, undermining my ability to feel grounded or hopeful about the future. I began to doubt my choices and my ability to overcome these challenges in a country that seemed determined to keep me on the margins.

The Isolation of Being an Outsider

Equally challenging was the isolation that came from feeling like an outsider. For all its openness, Germany often felt like a society closed to those who didn't conform to its norms. I struggled to fit into a culture where the rules and expectations were usually unspoken, and even the most minor social interactions seemed to carry hidden codes that I didn't fully understand. Whenever I encountered a cultural barrier, misinterpreted a gesture, or failed to pick up on a subtle social cue, it reinforced the sense that I was different and didn't belong.

The language barrier only intensified this isolation. While I had learned essential German, navigating conversations beyond simple exchanges was challenging. I found it difficult to express myself fully, connect with others on a deeper level, and build relationships beyond transactional interactions. Language, which should have been a bridge, felt like a wall, separating me from the community, from potential friendships, and a sense of belonging. This linguistic divide created a constant feeling of being on the outside looking in, watching life unfold around me without being able to participate fully.

The loneliness that came with this isolation was profound. In moments when I needed support when the weight of economic hardship felt too heavy to bear alone, I realized that I didn't have a strong network of people to lean on. Friendships were often superficial, limited by language and cultural differences, and my connections within the foreign community, while supportive, were also marked by a shared struggle for survival that left little room for genuine companionship. The isolation became a feedback loop, reinforcing feelings of inadequacy and disconnection, making reaching out, seeking comfort, and feeling understood harder.

Erosion of Self-Worth

One of the most insidious effects of these challenges was the erosion of my self-worth. Every rejection, every failed attempt at securing stable work, every unreturned call, or unacknowledged application felt like a personal failure. I began to internalize these setbacks, to believe that they were a reflection of my inadequacy rather than the result of a system that was inherently challenging for outsiders. I started to see myself through the lens of these rejections, questioning my abilities, worth, and value as a professional and person.

The constant hustle and the need to prove myself repeatedly took a toll on my confidence. No matter how many clients I secured or projects I completed, there was always a lingering sense that I was not enough, that I was falling short of the expectations that seemed to govern every aspect of life in Germany. This self-doubt became a shadow that followed me, a voice that questioned my every move, decision, and effort. The belief in my potential, in my capacity to succeed, became fragile, quickly shattered by even the most minor setback.

As my self-worth dwindled, I found it more challenging to advocate for myself, negotiate fair rates, and assert my value in professional settings. I felt I didn't have the right to demand more, as though I were an imposter in a world that was not mine. This lack of self-assurance affected every interaction, making me more susceptible to exploitation, more willing to accept low pay, and more likely to sacrifice my needs and boundaries to keep going. The erosion of my self-worth became a vicious cycle, where each compromise and concession only deepened my sense of inadequacy.

Mental Fatigue and Burnout

The constant economic pressure and the need to navigate an unwelcoming system led to a profound mental fatigue beyond physical exhaustion. Every day was a mental balancing act—calculating expenses, planning for uncertainties, managing relationships, and maintaining the energy to keep pushing forward despite setbacks. This mental strain took a toll on my well-being, leaving me feeling drained, depleted, and disconnected.

Burnout became a familiar companion, a state of emotional and psychological depletion that made even the most minor tasks feel overwhelming. There were days when I struggled to find the motivation to get out of bed, to face another day of uncertainty, another day of navigating a system that felt indifferent to my struggles. The constant mental strain made it difficult to experience joy, appreciate small victories, and find moments of peace. Everything became a blur of survival, a relentless drive to keep going that left little room for self-care or reflection.

This burnout affected my ability to think, to make decisions, and to trust my instincts. I second-guessed every choice, questioned my judgment, and wondered if I was making the right decisions or grasping at straws. The psychological toll of constant economic hardship made it hard to feel grounded, trust in my resilience, and belief in the possibility of a better future.

Identity Crisis and Loss of Purpose

Perhaps one of the most challenging aspects of this journey was the identity crisis that emerged due to these challenges. I came to Germany with a clear sense of who I was and what I wanted to achieve, but my circumstances forced me to question everything I thought I knew about myself. The roles I had once taken pride in—the skilled professional, the independent individual, the ambitious dreamer—began to feel distant, almost irrelevant, in the face of the daily grind of survival.

As I struggled to secure stable work and financial security, I felt as though I were losing parts of myself, the parts that had once defined my identity. I was no longer the person I had been, yet I hadn't become the person I had hoped to be. This in-between state, this liminal space, left me feeling unmoored, disconnected from a sense of purpose or direction. I began to wonder if my dreams were misguided, if the goals I had set for myself were unrealistic if the vision I had for my future was nothing more than a fantasy.

The loss of identity was perhaps the most painful aspect of this psychological journey. I felt like I had become a stranger to myself, someone going through the motions, driven by necessity rather than passion or purpose. The economic challenges had stripped away the layers of who I thought I was, leaving me vulnerable, exposed, and uncertain of who I was becoming. This identity crisis deepened the shadow of doubt that lingered over me, a reminder that the journey to stability was not only a test of resilience but a confrontation with the very core of who I was.

Resilience Amidst the Shadows

Despite the profound psychological impact of these challenges, a part of me remained resilient, a tiny spark that refused to be extinguished. In moments of despair, I would remind myself why I had come to Germany, the dreams that had induced my journey, and the hope that had kept me going. This resilience wasn't loud or grand; it was quiet, persistent, a refusal to give up even when everything felt impossible.

This inner strength became my anchor, a source of comfort amidst the chaos, a reminder that I could endure, adapt, and find my way even in the darkest moments. The psychological toll was confirmed; the shadows of doubt were heavy, but so was my resolve to keep moving forward. I knew that the journey would not be easy and the challenges would continue, but I also knew that I was more potent than the obstacles I faced and that my identity, worth, and purpose were not defined by the hardships alone.

Resilience and Purpose

Resilience isn't something that comes all at once; it's built piece by piece, forged in the fires of hardship and tempered by each struggle that threatens to break you. When I first arrived in Germany, I had no idea of the journey ahead, no understanding of how challenging it would be to navigate a life in a foreign country where every step forward seemed to come with a setback. Yet, as each obstacle appeared, as each struggle tested my will, I discovered a part of myself that I hadn't known before—a sense of resilience that grew with each experience, a strength that became my anchor. Over time, these struggles began to shape my life's purpose, clarify what mattered most, and sow the seeds of an unbreakable will to continue.

Learning to Endure

At first, resilience felt like nothing more than the ability to endure and withstand the hardships that came my way without allowing them to defeat me. Each setback—whether a rejected job application, a cancel gig, or another bureaucratic hurdle—was an opportunity to either give in to frustration or find a way forward. I learned early on that giving up was not an option; the life I had envisioned would not materialize if I let these challenges overwhelm me.

Endurance became a daily practice, a commitment to push through even when the weight of uncertainty felt unbearable. Each time I encountered an obstacle, I reminded myself that this was part of the journey and that success was not meant to come quickly, especially not in an environment as structured and challenging as Germany's. This mindset allowed me to see each struggle as a temporary hardship rather than a permanent defeat. Over time, I found that the more I endured, the stronger I became. Endurance wasn't just about surviving each day; it was about building the foundation of resilience, a mental and emotional fortitude that would sustain me for the long haul.

The experience of learning to endure also gave me a new perspective on what it meant to work toward a goal. In the past, I had often focused on immediate results, expecting success to follow quickly after effort. But in Germany, I realized that this mindset wouldn't serve me. Here, progress was incremental, each step forward hard-earned and painstakingly slow. Endurance taught me to value the journey and understand that genuine growth comes from persistence and the commitment to keep moving even when the destination feels distant.

Finding Strength in Adaptability

Resilience also demanded adaptability, an ability to adjust my approach, mindset, and expectations in response to the challenges I faced. Germany's economic system, bureaucratic structure, and cultural norms required a level of flexibility I hadn't anticipated. Each time I encountered a roadblock, I was forced to go through all over again, find a new strategy, and adapt in ways that allowed me to keep moving forward.

Adapting wasn't always easy; it often meant letting go of familiar routines, comfortable habits, and even parts of my identity. I had to learn new ways of communicating, new ways of working, and new ways of presenting myself. But this adaptability became a source of strength. Each adjustment and change in perspective made me more resilient and capable of handling the unexpected. I began to see adaptability not as a concession but as a skill, a way of navigating the world that allowed me to survive and thrive in initially unwelcoming environments.

Through these experiences, I learned that resilience is not about rigidly holding onto a single path; it's about finding multiple paths, about having the flexibility to shift directions without losing sight of the ultimate goal. This adaptability gave me a sense of agency, a feeling that, even if I couldn't control every aspect of my environment, I could control how I responded. In a place where so much felt uncertain, this adaptability became a source of empowerment, a reminder that I could shape my journey.

Redefining Success and Purpose

As I navigated life's challenges in Germany, I found myself rethinking my definition of success. Initially, I had come here with specific goals—a stable job, financial security, and a sense of belonging. However, as each setback forced me to start from scratch, I realized that success was not simply about achieving these external milestones. I discovered that true success was about resilience, the ability to continue pursuing a goal despite the obstacles, and maintaining hope even when progress was slow.

This shift in perspective allowed me to find purpose in the struggle itself. Rather than viewing each setback as a failure, I started to see it as part of a more extensive journey, a path teaching me valuable lessons about perseverance, humility, and inner strength. My purpose became less about reaching a specific destination and more about becoming someone who could withstand the journey, face hardship without losing hope, and keep going even when the odds seemed stacked against me.

This newfound purpose gave me a sense of clarity, a direction rooted in resilience rather than external achievement. I realized that my journey was not just about building a life in Germany but a life of strength, resilience, and meaning. This purpose became my guiding light, a source of motivation that kept me grounded in moments of doubt, a reminder that every challenge was an opportunity to grow, become more robust, and deepen my sense of purpose.

Developing Inner Strength Through Vulnerability

Resilience also required me to confront my vulnerabilities and acknowledge the doubts, fears, and insecurities that came with each hardship. At first, I saw vulnerability as a weakness, something to hide or suppress to appear strong. But as the challenges grew, I realized that resilience wasn't about denying vulnerability—it was about embracing it, about understanding that true strength comes from facing these inner struggles head-on.

Allowing myself to be vulnerable and admit that I was struggling was a difficult but necessary part of the journey. I found that vulnerability made me more compassionate toward myself, forgiving my mistakes and accepting that I was a work in progress. This self-compassion became a critical component of my resilience, a reminder that I didn't have to be perfect and could continue moving forward even if I stumbled along the way.

Vulnerability also opened the door to deeper connections with others. As I allowed myself to share my struggles, I found that others were more willing to support me, offer advice, and listen. These connections reminded me that resilience isn't a solitary struggle; it grows within a community through shared experiences, mutual support, and the understanding that we are all navigating our challenges. By embracing vulnerability, I discovered a new kind of strength—one grounded in authenticity, in the courage to face myself as I was.

Resilience as a Lifelong Practice

Over time, I understood that resilience is not a destination; it's a lifelong practice, a mindset that must be cultivated daily. Each new challenge and setback allowed me to strengthen this mindset and build upon the resilience I had already developed. I learned to view resilience as a skill that could be refined and improved, and I grew more robust with each experience.

This resilience practice became a habit, a way of approaching life that emphasized persistence, adaptability, and hope. Even when the obstacles felt overwhelming, and doubt threatened to consume me, I reminded myself that resilience was about moving forward, one step at a time. I didn't need all the answers to know exactly how everything would unfold; I just needed to keep going and trust that my resilience would guide me.

Each time I faced a new hardship, I drew upon this practice, using the lessons I had learned to navigate the present moment. Resilience became my anchor, a source of stability that allowed me to weather the storms and remain grounded even when everything around me felt uncertain. This practice taught me that resilience is not a single act of strength; it's a continuous commitment, a choice to keep going despite hardships and to believe in the possibility of a better future even when the present is filled with struggle.

An Unbreakable Will to Continue

The cumulative effect of these experiences was an unbreakable will to continue, a determination forged in the fires of hardship and tempered by each struggle. I realized that I had developed a strength that went beyond the challenges of living in Germany; it was a resilience that would stay with me, a will that could withstand any obstacle. This unbreakable will become my most significant asset, a source of confidence that reminds me of my ability to persevere, overcome, and create a life of meaning and purpose regardless of the circumstances.

This will to continue wasn't just about survival; it was about thriving, finding ways to grow, evolve, and become the person I wanted to be. Each struggle had given me a gift—a deeper understanding of myself, a greater appreciation for resilience, a clearer sense of purpose. These lessons strengthened my will, transforming doubt into determination, uncertainty into clarity, and hardship into hope.

As I looked back on my journey, I realized that every sacrifice, every setback, and every moment of doubt had contributed to this unbreakable will. My struggles were not merely obstacles but the building blocks of my resilience, the foundation of a strength that could endure any hardship. This will continue becoming the essence of who I was, a testament to the resilience I had cultivated, a reminder that I could achieve the life I had envisioned.

Purpose Redefined: Resilience as the Path Forward

Ultimately, these struggles led me to redefine my purpose and see resilience as a means of survival and a path forward. I understood that my journey in Germany was about more than economic stability or personal success; it was about cultivating a resilience that could carry me through any challenge, a strength that would allow me to create a life of meaning and fulfillment. This purpose became my guiding force, a source of motivation that kept me grounded, hopeful, and committed to the journey ahead.

In the end, resilience became more than just a skill; it became a way of life, a mindset that allowed me to face each new day with courage, determination, and an unbreakable will to continue. This resilience, this sense of purpose, was the greatest gift that my struggles had given me—a reminder that, no matter how difficult the journey, I had the strength to keep going, to rise above, to create a life defined not by hardship, but by resilience and purpose.

Chapter 5
Light Beyond the Shadows

AFTER MONTHS OF RELENTLESS hustle, sacrifices, and the psychological toll of uncertainty, I began to experience moments like rays of light breaking through the dense shadows. They weren't grand milestones but small, hard-won successes with profound meaning. Each one reminded me that, despite the challenges, progress was possible. These early victories were glimmers of hope, sparks that reignited my belief in myself and my purpose, showing me that even the darkest journeys hold moments of light. These small successes were the beginnings of something more, signs that my resilience was bearing fruit.

The First Breakthrough: Securing Stable Work

Finding stable work was one of the first breakthroughs that brought a renewed sense of hope. Until then, my employment had been a patchwork of gigs and informal jobs, none of which provided the security or consistency I desperately needed. While freelancing in Germany's shadow economy allowed me to get by, it was exhausting and emotionally draining. The unpredictability kept me in a state of constant anxiety, and I longed for the stability that came with a steady income.

After months of searching, applying, and enduring countless rejections, I finally secured a position that provided both regular hours and a reliable Pay-check. It wasn't a high-level role, nor was it in my preferred field, but it offered the one thing I had craved since arriving: stability. The job was at a small company that welcomed diverse backgrounds, and they appreciated my work ethic and dedication. For the first time, I could relax slightly, to feel a foundation beneath me, even if it was still fragile.

That first Pay-check was more than just money; it validated my journey and reminded me that perseverance could yield results. It allowed me to begin planning, start building modest savings, and worry less about whether I could cover rent each month. It was a small victory that brought a renewed sense of hope. I no longer felt like I was scrambling in the dark; I had taken my first natural step toward stability, which gave me the strength to keep pushing forward.

A Breakthrough Project: Proving My Worth

While stable work brought relief, it was a breakthrough project that reminded me of my capabilities and reignited my confidence. A client approached me through a referral, someone who had heard about my skills and was looking for someone to take on a significant project. This client needed a website redesign and marketing strategy, and after our initial conversation, I could tell they were impressed by my knowledge and vision. For the first time, I felt recognized and seen for what I could truly offer, and I was determined to make the most of this opportunity.

The project was demanding, requiring countless hours of design work, research, and late nights. I poured myself into every detail, determined to exceed expectations and prove to my client and myself that I was capable of delivering exceptional results. As the project progressed, my client's feedback was positive, each compliment and expression of satisfaction making of line to my determination to see it through.

When I completed the project, my client was thrilled with the results, and they even referred me to others within their network. That referral was a turning point, a tangible validation of my skills and resilience. It opened doors to more projects, clients, and opportunities, each bringing a renewed sense of hope and a reminder that I had something valuable to offer. This project became a beacon, a reminder that, despite the setbacks, my efforts were making a difference. It was a breakthrough that renewed my sense of purpose and motivation.

A Meaningful Connection: Finding a Friend and Mentor

Amid my hustle, I met someone who would become an ally, mentor, and friend. Her name was Sarah, an expat from another country living in Germany for years. Sarah was well-established, having faced many of the same challenges I was experiencing, and she had successfully navigated the complexities of life in Germany's demanding economic system. We met at a networking event for international professionals, and from our first conversation, we had a natural rapport.

Sarah understood my struggles in a way few others did. She shared stories of her journey, the moments of doubt, the countless rejections, and the small victories that had kept her going. Her empathy and insights became a source of strength, reminding me that I wasn't alone. Sarah was interested in my progress, offering practical advice and connecting me with people within her network. She became a guiding light who believed in me and encouraged me to keep striving for my goals.

Through Sarah, I found both a friend and a mentor, someone who could provide the support I needed to grow. Her belief in me was transformative; it gave me a renewed sense of confidence and a feeling that I was part of a larger community of foreigners who had carved out their paths. Knowing that someone with experience and knowledge saw potential in me validated my efforts. It reminded me that resilience was about enduring and finding those who could help me along the way.

The First Sense of Belonging

As I began to secure more stable work and build a modest network, I felt something I hadn't felt since arriving in Germany: a sense of belonging. It was subtle at first—small moments of connection, recognition, and feeling seen. For so long, I had felt like an outsider, navigating a world that didn't seem to have a place for me. But as I built relationships, secured work, and established myself, I felt like I was slowly finding my footing.

This sense of belonging was amplified when some of my clients and colleagues invited me to a gathering. The gathering was a mix of locals and internationals, and for the first time, I felt at ease in a social setting. I could communicate, share my experiences, and converse without feeling like an outsider. Though still new and fragile, these connections made me think that perhaps I was beginning to carve out a space for myself in Germany.

These moments of belonging, of feeling included, have brought a renewed faith in my journey. They reminded me that while the road had been burdensome, it was not impossible. The early successes—the stable work, the breakthrough project, the meaningful connections—were proof that I could create a life here and find my place even in a country that had once felt impenetrable.

Building Momentum: The Power of Small Wins

These small successes—finding stable work, completing a significant project, forming meaningful connections—added up over time, creating a sense of momentum that had been absent initially. These early wins, while modest, gave me a foundation to build upon, a sense of progress that went full steam ahead my resilience. I no longer felt as though I was constantly struggling to survive; I felt as though I was beginning to thrive, to create something meaningful and sustainable.

My confidence grew with each new project, connection, and small victory. I began to set larger goals, dream bigger, and envision a future no longer defined by hardship alone. The shadows of doubt still lingered, but they no longer held the same power over me. I had proven to myself that I was capable, could succeed, and that my efforts were not in vain. This momentum became a source of hope, a reminder that resilience was paying off and that each step forward brought me closer to the life I had envisioned.

Renewed Faith in My Journey

These early successes brought something even more important than stability or progress—they brought renewed faith in my journey. For so long, I had questioned whether I was on the right path, whether my dreams were realistic, and whether I would ever find a sense of purpose and belonging in Germany. But these small victories, these moments of light beyond the shadows, reminded me that my journey had meaning and that each struggle was part of a larger story.

This renewed faith became a wellspring of resilience and inner strength that allowed me to face new challenges with optimism and purpose. I was no longer defined by the hardships alone; I was defined by my ability to overcome them, find hope in the smallest moments, and keep moving forward even when the road was difficult. No matter how modest, each success was a testament to my resilience, a reminder that I could create a life of meaning and purpose.

As I reflected on these early successes, I realized they were more than just accomplishments; they were symbols of my growth, resilience, and unbreakable will to continue. They reminded me that while the journey had been filled with shadows, there was light beyond them, a life of hope and possibility waiting to be built. These small wins were not the end of my struggles, but they were proof that my journey was worth pursuing and that each step forward brought me closer to the life I had dreamed of.

Ultimately, these light moments became a source of strength, a reminder that even the darkest journeys hold moments of beauty and hope. Each success, each connection, each sense of belonging was a beacon, a guide that led me through the shadows and showed me the way forward. And with each new victory, no matter how small, I was reminded that resilience was not just about enduring hardship; it was about finding the light beyond the shadows, about creating a life defined not by struggle alone but by hope, purpose, and unyielding strength.

Lessons in Adaptation

When I first arrived in Germany, I quickly realized that thriving here would require more than hard work and determination; it would demand adaptation at a profound level. I had to become more than just an observer of German culture—I needed to immerse myself in it to learn its language, customs, and unspoken social and economic codes. Each step toward understanding these elements was a lesson in humility, patience, and resilience. Adapting was a gradual process requiring constant learning, unlearning, and relearning as I began to see the world through a new lens. The journey to adaptation was not easy, but it transformed me, teaching me the skills and mindset necessary to thrive in a land that was initially foreign and, at times, unwelcoming.

The Language Barrier: Overcoming Isolation and Opening Doors

Learning German was my first major challenge and one of the most critical steps toward adaptation. Language is more than just a tool for communication; it's a key to culture, a way of connecting with others and understanding the nuances that shape daily interactions. When I first arrived, my limited German skills left me feeling isolated, like a spectator watching life unfold around me without being able to participate fully. I knew that if I wanted to integrate and belong genuinely, I needed to speak the language at a basic level and fluently enough to navigate both personal and professional spaces.

My initial attempts at learning German were humbling. The grammar was complex, the vocabulary vast, and the pronunciation unfamiliar. I often felt frustrated, as if I were starting over from scratch, struggling to express even simple thoughts. But I persevered, attending language classes, practicing with anyone patient enough to listen, and immersing myself in German media—reading newspapers, watching local TV shows, and listening to German podcasts. Each interaction, each conversation, was a small victory, a step toward bridging the gap that separated me from those around me.

As my language skills improved, I began to notice subtle changes. Conversations with locals became easier, interactions at work more fluid, and I could pick up on Joy, irony, and other nuances that had previously gone over my head. Learning the language wasn't just about understanding words; it was about understanding people, about seeing the world through a German lens. This newfound linguistic ability gave me confidence, a feeling that I was no longer an outsider but someone who could engage meaningfully, contribute to conversations, and connect with others on a deeper level. Language became a bridge, transforming my interactions and allowing me to navigate social spaces with greater ease and understanding.

Understanding Social Etiquette: The Unspoken Rules of Interaction

In Germany, social interactions follow unspoken rules that take time to grasp. Unlike the casual, spontaneous interactions I was used to, German social etiquette is rooted in formality, directness, and respect for personal boundaries. The first lesson I learned was the importance of punctuality. In Germany, being on time is not just appreciated—it's expected. Arriving a few minutes late can be considered disrespectful, an unspoken breach of trust. At first, this felt restrictive, but over time, I realized the predictability and reliability that punctuality brought to interactions.

Another aspect of German social etiquette is the value placed on directness. In my culture, communication often involves nuance, subtlety, and indirect phrasing to avoid conflict or offense. But in Germany, people value honesty and clarity, even if it may seem blunt. I had to adjust my communication style, learning to be more straightforward in my interactions with colleagues, clients, or even friends. This directness initially felt uncomfortable, as though I were being overly assertive. Still, I understood that in Germany, clarity is seen as a sign of respect, a way of ensuring mutual understanding and efficiency.

Adapting to these unspoken social rules required me to observe, listen, and learn from my mistakes. There were times when I unintentionally overstepped boundaries when my cultural norms clashed with German expectations. But each misstep was a learning experience, a reminder that adaptation is a process of trial and error. I gradually began to feel more comfortable and confident in my interactions as I learned to navigate the subtle dance of German social etiquette.

Decoding Workplace Culture: Hierarchy, Efficiency, and Team Dynamics

The workplace presented its own set of challenges and unspoken rules that I had to adapt to. German workplace culture is known for its formality, structured hierarchy, and focus on efficiency. Unlike the more relaxed, collaborative environments I had been used to, the German workplace demanded a clear understanding of roles, respect for authority, and a commitment to productivity.

One of the first lessons I learned was the importance of hierarchy. In many workplaces, titles are respected, and there is a clear distinction between management and employees. Decision-making is often centralized, with higher-ups having the final say on important matters. Initially, this hierarchical structure felt rigid, almost intimidating, as I was used to environments where input from all levels was encouraged. Over time, I learned to respect this structure and understand that it was a system designed to ensure order and accountability. Rather than resisting it, I adapted by respecting authority, understanding the chain of command, and learning to express my ideas within the boundaries of this structure.

Efficiency and productivity are also highly valued in the German workplace. Meetings are concise, agendas are followed strictly, and there is little tolerance for unnecessary small talk. This focus on efficiency took some adjustment, as I was accustomed to workplaces where social interactions played a significant role in team building. I had to learn to communicate concisely, stay focused on the task, and respect others' time by being prepared and organized. This adaptation improved my professional relationships and my productivity, teaching me the value of clear goals, time management, and task prioritization.

Team dynamics were another area where adaptation was essential. In Germany, professional relationships are formal, especially in the beginning. Building trust takes time, and personal matters are usually kept separate from work. I learned to approach my colleagues professionally, respect their privacy, and understand that trust would develop gradually. This formal approach differed from the more immediate camaraderie I was used to. Still, it helped me understand the importance of boundaries and professionalism in a way I hadn't before.

Navigating Bureaucracy: Patience and Precision as Survival Skills

Germany's bureaucratic system is known for its complexity, and adapting to it required patience and precision that was both challenging and rewarding. Bureaucracy here is deeply embedded in daily life, from securing housing and health insurance to registering your address and paying taxes. Each process has specific requirements; even the most minor mistake can result in delays, additional paperwork, or rejection.

At first, the bureaucracy was overwhelming. Every task required an endless list of documents, forms, and appointments, each meticulously detailed and unforgiving of errors. I learned early on that patience was essential. Rushing through forms or skipping steps only led to more complications. Instead, I developed a systematic approach, double-checking each document, following instructions precisely, and preparing extra copies of everything just in case.

Precision became my survival skill. I learned to pay attention to every detail, to anticipate potential issues, and to approach each bureaucratic task with a sense of thoroughness. This level of precision taught me a new kind of discipline, a respect for systems and structures that, while rigid, were designed to ensure order. I understood that in Germany, bureaucracy is a way of maintaining stability, reflecting the country's commitment to reliability and accountability. By adapting to this system and learning to work within its constraints, I could navigate it more effectively, avoid unnecessary setbacks, and build a sense of stability within my own life.

Understanding Economic Norms: Financial Discipline and Long-Term Planning

Adapting to Germany's economic norms required a shift in mindset, particularly around financial discipline and long-term planning. In Germany, financial stability is highly valued, and there is an emphasis on careful budgeting, saving, and responsible spending. This approach to finances differed from what I was used to, where short-term gains and immediate needs often took precedence.

Learning to manage my finances in a way that aligned with German norms required me to develop a new level of financial discipline. I created a budget, meticulously tracked my income and expenses, and prioritized saving even when my earnings were modest. This financial discipline was initially challenging, requiring sacrifices and a commitment to delaying gratification. But over time, I saw the benefits of this approach. Saving gave me a sense of security, a cushion that allowed me to weather unexpected expenses without feeling destabilized. Financial discipline became a form of empowerment, a way of controlling my economic circumstances in a country where financial stability is a cornerstone of success.

Long-term planning was another adjustment. In Germany, people tend to think in terms of decades, planning not only for the immediate future but for retirement, potential health needs, and family stability. I began to see the value in setting long-term goals and thinking beyond the next few months or years. This shift in perspective encouraged me to invest in myself and think about the skills, relationships, and financial decisions that would serve me in the future. It was an adaptation that gave me a sense of purpose, a roadmap that extended beyond survival and toward a life of stability and growth.

Building a Support Network: Trust and Community

Adapting to life in Germany wasn't just about learning systems and structures and finding a sense of community. Building a support network was essential, but it required time, patience, and a willingness to step outside my comfort zone. Trust is earned gradually in Germany, and friendships often develop over shared experiences rather than immediate connections.

Through language classes, networking events, and community gatherings, I began to meet people who understood my journey, both locals and fellow foreigners. These connections provided not only practical support but also emotional resilience. I found mentors who offered guidance, friends who provided companionship, and allies who shared resources and advice. Building this network taught me the importance of trust, mutual support, and showing up for others as they showed up for me.

Over time, this support network became a foundation, a reminder that I wasn't alone in my journey. These relationships enriched my life, teaching me the value of patience, empathy, and community. Adapting to Germany's social norms didn't mean losing my identity; it meant integrating and finding a balance between my culture and the one I was now part of. This network became a source of strength, a light that guided me through the challenges, a community that reminded me that adaptation wasn't just about survival; it was about thriving, about finding a place where I could belong.

Conclusion: Adaptation as Transformation

The journey of adaptation transformed me in ways I hadn't anticipated. Each lesson—learning the language, understanding social etiquette, navigating the workplace, managing finances, and building a support network—was a step toward integration, making Germany feel less foreign and more like home. This adaptation wasn't about losing myself; it was about evolving, about becoming someone who could navigate multiple worlds with resilience, grace, and purpose.

Through these lessons, I discovered that adaptation is not a single act but an ongoing process, a way of engaging with the world that requires humility, openness, and a willingness to grow. Each adaptation was a testament to my resilience, a reminder that I could thrive in an environment that had once felt overwhelming. The journey wasn't easy, but it was transformative. It taught me that proper adaptation is about embracing change, finding strength in flexibility, and creating a life of meaning and belonging, even in the face of challenges. In the end, adaptation became more than a survival skill—a way of life, a path toward a future I could call my own.

Embracing Duality

Germany offered a new life and a promise of stability but also presented more profound challenges than I had anticipated. In a place where I hoped to find opportunity, I discovered a world with obstacles—some visible, others unspoken. While the struggle to integrate was intense, so were the rewards when I succeeded. Over time,

I lived in two realities: the experience of being an outsider, never fully understood or integrated, and a growing sense of belonging that allowed me to create a life on my terms. Embracing this duality—of holding both struggle and opportunity, of accepting that I could be both a part of German society and set apart from it—ultimately allowed me to build a sense of peace, a way to live authentically within the paradox.

The Hope of Opportunity and the Reality of Struggle

When I arrived in Germany, I was filled with hope and determination. I knew that Germany had a reputation for opportunity, economic stability, and providing a chance to build a life that could weather the world's uncertainties. I had heard stories of people who had come to Germany and created fulfilling lives, and I believed that with hard work, I could do the same. But as I began my journey, the path was far from straightforward. I encountered barriers that were as invisible as they were real—bureaucratic obstacles, language difficulties, and an unspoken sense that I didn't quite belong.

The paradox of opportunity and struggle was evident in every aspect of my life. On the one hand, there were clear possibilities: a stable economy, social services that provided a safety net, and a society that valued order and discipline. On the other hand, there was a labyrinth of systems that seemed designed to test my endurance and remind me of my outsider status—applying for jobs required not only qualifications but a deep understanding of the German language and cultural norms. Securing housing meant navigating complex bureaucratic processes and often needed a level of financial history in Germany that was impossible to establish overnight.

Each barrier was a reminder that while opportunity existed, it was conditional—it required adaptation, patience, and the willingness to accept struggle as a part of the process. I began to realize that struggle was not something to avoid or overcome but something to embrace, to see as part of the journey. With each hurdle, I found myself growing, adapting, and learning about German society and my resilience. This shift in perspective allowed me to view struggle not as an enemy but as a teacher, a necessary counterpart to the opportunities I sought.

Finding Peace in the Space Between Cultures

As I navigated the practical challenges of building a life in Germany, I also faced the more subtle internal struggle of existing between two cultures. My cultural background had shaped my values, way of communicating, and understanding of community; yet, to fully integrate into German society, I had to learn to adopt new norms and ways of thinking and behaving. I felt pulled in two directions: the desire to hold onto my identity and blend into a society that valued structure, precision, and directness.

This sense of cultural duality was disorienting at first. In my culture, relationships, and interactions were often defined by warmth, subtlety, and indirectness—qualities that contrasted sharply with the German emphasis on straightforwardness, punctuality, and personal boundaries. I struggled with this difference, sometimes feeling caught between two opposing worlds. I wanted to connect with those around me, to feel a sense of belonging, but I didn't want to lose the parts of myself that felt integral to who I was.

Over time, I began to see that this duality was not something to overcome but to embrace. I could be both: I could hold onto my own cultural identity while respecting and adapting to the norms of German society. I learned to navigate social interactions with a balance of both approaches, allowing myself to be direct when necessary and bringing warmth and subtlety to my relationships. This balance allowed me to find a sense of peace, a way to exist authentically within a familiar and foreign society.

The Insider-Outsider Paradox

One of the most profound aspects of my experience in Germany was the feeling of being both an insider and an outsider. At times, I felt fully integrated, able to navigate the systems, speak the language, and participate in the daily rhythms of German life. In other moments, I felt acutely aware of my differences, reminded by subtle cues that I was not truly "German." This dual status was empowering and isolating—a reminder of how far I had come and the limits of integration.

The experience of being an outsider was often painful, particularly in situations where I felt excluded or misunderstood. I would notice how people looked at me, the subtle hesitations in their voices when they realized I was a foreigner, and the way conversations would sometimes shift to more superficial topics or fewer questions as if my background made a more profound connection impossible. These experiences were reminders that, no matter how much I adapted, there would always be a part of me that was set apart and shaped by a culture and identity different from the majority.

Yet, there were also moments when I felt included and my efforts to integrate were acknowledged and respected. I began to find peace in this duality, realizing that I could be both an outsider and an insider; I didn't have to choose between them. I could exist in this space of duality, finding fulfillment in the balance of both perspectives. This acceptance allowed me to navigate my life in Germany with a sense of fluidity, a recognition that I could belong without sacrificing my identity.

Learning to Live with Ambiguity

One of the most valuable lessons I learned was the importance of embracing ambiguity. In my journey to adapt to Germany, I constantly questioned who I was, where I belonged, and what success meant in this new context. I had come to Germany with a clear vision of what I wanted to achieve, but the reality was much more complex. Each step forward came with new uncertainties and new questions that challenged my understanding of myself and my purpose.

I learned that ambiguity was not something to resist but to accept and allow as part of the journey. I didn't need to have all the answers; I didn't need to define my place within German society fully. I could live in the in-between, finding peace in the uncertainty, understanding that my journey was not about reaching a single destination but continually evolving and growing. This acceptance of ambiguity brought a sense of freedom, a release from the pressure to fit neatly into one identity or culture. I could be both, or neither, or somewhere in between, and that was enough.

Redefining Success and Belonging

I embraced this duality and began redefining my understanding of success and belonging. Initially, I had equated success with complete integration, with reaching a point where I felt entirely accepted and understood. But as I adapted, I realized that success was not about fitting in perfectly but finding my path and creating a meaningful and fulfilling life, even if it didn't conform to conventional definitions of belonging.

Belonging, I discovered, was not about erasing my differences or conforming entirely to German norms; it was about creating connections, building relationships, and finding spaces where I could feel at home. I found belonging in moments of mutual understanding, friendships that transcended cultural differences, and communities that valued diversity. These connections allowed me to see belonging as something that could exist alongside my outsider status, as a space where I could be both integrated and unique.

This redefined sense of success and belonging gave me a renewed sense of purpose. I no longer felt the need to achieve a specific level of acceptance or recognition; I was content with the journey itself, the process of adapting and growing, and creating an authentic and fulfilling life.

Embracing Duality as a Source of Strength

Ultimately, embracing duality became a source of strength, a way of navigating the complexities of life in Germany with resilience and grace. I learned that I could hold multiple truths at once—that I could be both a part of German society and separate from it, that I could face struggle and still find opportunity, that I could exist in the in-between and still feel whole. This duality was not a contradiction but a reflection of my journey, a testament to my ability to adapt, find peace in uncertainty, and create a life of meaning within the paradox.

This acceptance of duality allowed me to live more fully and engage with my experiences without categorizing or resolving them. I could see the beauty in the contradictions, the moments of connection and isolation, the challenges that shaped my resilience, and the opportunities that inspired my hope. Embracing duality became not just a way of surviving but a way of thriving and finding strength in the complexities of my identity, my journey, and my life in Germany.

Chapter 6
Rising in the Land of Shadows

LIVING AS A FOREIGNER in Germany meant facing a series of uphill battles, each testing my resilience, adaptability, and commitment to my dreams. Yet, amid the obstacles and the shadows of doubt, there were moments of triumph—significant milestones that marked my journey and proved that perseverance could yield success. These milestones, each a hard-won victory, were not just achievements; they were testaments to my growth, a reminder that even in the most challenging environments, it is possible to rise and create a life filled with purpose, stability, and fulfillment. Each milestone brought a sense of accomplishment, a feeling of having reached new heights despite the odds.

Career Milestone: Securing My First Major Role

One of the most defining moments in my journey was securing my first significant role in Germany. This position provided financial stability and marked a turning point in my career. Until then, I had been working temporary or freelance jobs, piecing together work wherever I could. The instability was emotionally and financially exhausting, and I knew that finding a permanent role would be essential for building the life I envisioned.

After months of applying, facing rejections, and honing my skills, I finally landed an interview for a position that felt perfect. The role aligned with my experience and aspirations, allowing me to work in a field I was passionate about. I prepared meticulously for the interview, knowing this opportunity could change everything. Walking into that interview room was nerve-wracking, but I felt ready. I was prepared to demonstrate my professional skills, commitment, and adaptability, which kept me moving forward despite the challenges.

When I received the job offer, it felt surreal. This position wasn't just a job; it was a validation of my journey, a recognition of my skills, and a breakthrough that represented years of perseverance. The role provided me with financial stability, professional growth, and a sense of belonging within a team that valued my contributions. It was a milestone that marked my transition from surviving to thriving, a moment when I felt I had genuinely risen above the shadows that had once seemed so overwhelming.

Personal Milestone: Establishing a Sense of Belonging

Another significant milestone was finding a sense of belonging that had felt elusive for so long. As a foreigner, I often felt like an outsider, navigating a society where integration was challenging, and I constantly had to prove my place. Over time, I built connections, formed friendships, and learned to navigate the social landscape of Germany. These relationships, each one a small victory in itself, culminated in a sense of community—a feeling that I was no longer just a visitor but a part of something larger.

One defining moment came when I was invited to a celebration by a local friend, a gathering that included both Germans and internationals. Being included in this group and welcomed into their traditions and festivals were powerful reminders of my progress. I was no longer simply navigating the periphery; I was part of the fabric of this community. That evening, surrounded by friends and laughter, I felt a sense of peace that I had carved out a place for myself in Germany.

This milestone was not about a specific achievement but about reaching a point of acceptance, a recognition that I belonged here in my way. It was a feeling of integration beyond language skills or cultural knowledge—an emotional milestone, a reminder that I was no longer a stranger but a valued community member. This sense of belonging gave me a newfound confidence, a foundation of support that would continue to sustain me in the years to come.

Financial Milestone: Achieving Stability and Independence

Achieving financial stability was one of the most transformative milestones in my journey. When I first arrived in Germany, financial insecurity was a constant worry. Living Pay-check to Pay-check, I often wondered if I'd ever be able to build a stable life. Every expense felt like a potential crisis, and every financial decision came with a sense of fear and uncertainty. My goal was not just to survive but to reach a point where I could live with dignity, where financial independence was within my grasp.

Over time, through careful budgeting, hard work, and smart financial choices, I began to see progress. Securing a stable role in my career was a significant turning point, allowing me to create a foundation upon which I could build financial security. With each Salary, I could set aside a portion for savings, slowly building a safety net to protect me from the uncertainties I had once feared.

The day I realized that I was financially stable was a quiet but profound milestone. I remember looking at my bank balance and seeing a savings buffer that provided a sense of security I hadn't felt in years. It was a moment of liberation—a recognition that I had created a life where financial hardship was no longer a constant shadow and I could plan for the future with confidence and autonomy. This achievement wasn't just about money; it was about freedom, about knowing that I could rely on myself and that I had risen above the economic challenges that had once defined my experience in Germany.

Cultural Milestone: Navigating Bureaucracy with Confidence

Germany's bureaucracy is notorious for its complexity, and navigating this system as a foreigner was one of my most significant challenges. Early on, every encounter with the bureaucracy felt overwhelming, as though I were being tested at every turn. Language barriers, complex paperwork, and the need for meticulous precision made each interaction a daunting experience. I often felt lost, unsure how to approach each new requirement, and fearful of making mistakes that could set me back.

But with time, I became more adept at navigating the system. I learned the importance of preparation, double-checking every document, and patiently approaching each interaction. I also learned to advocate for myself, ask questions, seek clarification when necessary, and stand my ground when faced with challenges. This process of learning and adapting gave me a sense of empowerment, a feeling that I could navigate even the most daunting systems with resilience and confidence.

The day I completed a complex bureaucratic process—securing a long-term visa, finalizing my health insurance, or completing a tax filing without outside help—was a milestone. It marked a shift from feeling helpless and intimidated to feeling capable and self-assured. This achievement was not just a practical victory but a symbol of my growth, a testament to my ability to adapt and thrive within a system that had once felt impenetrable. This milestone represented my transition from being overwhelmed by bureaucracy to mastering it, a significant step toward building a life of independence and stability.

Professional Milestone: Receiving Recognition and Promotion

As my career progressed, one of the most meaningful milestones was receiving recognition for my work, which validated my skills and the journey I had undertaken to establish myself in Germany. Being recognized for my contributions was more than just a professional achievement; it was a personal victory, a reminder that my hard work had not gone unnoticed.

After years of dedication, I was offered a promotion. This position not only came with increased responsibilities but also allowed me to lead projects, mentor new team members, and significantly impact the organization. This promotion was a milestone that represented years of perseverance, a testament to my resilience and my commitment to excellence. It reminded me that, despite the challenges of being a foreigner in Germany, I could succeed on my terms.

The promotion gave me a renewed sense of purpose, a feeling that I contributed meaningfully to the organization and my professional growth. It was a recognition that I was surviving and thriving and had built a respected and valued career. This milestone was a turning point, a reminder that success was possible even in the face of adversity and that I could rise above the shadows and create a fulfilling life of purpose and achievement.

Personal Milestone: Creating a Home

One of the most profound milestones in my journey was when I realized that Germany had become my home. This sense of home wasn't defined by a single event but by a series of small, meaningful moments that accumulated over time. It was in the friendships I had built, the routines I had established, and the familiar streets and cafes that had become part of my daily life. It was in the sense of peace I felt walking through my area, in the comfort of returning to a truly mine-space.

Creating a home was one of the most significant achievements, as it represented a sense of belonging that had once felt elusive. I had transformed a foreign place into a sanctuary, a space that reflected my identity, my journey, and my resilience. This milestone was about more than just finding a place to live; it was about creating a life that felt rooted, a life that was built on the foundation of all the struggles and successes I had experienced.

Reaching this milestone gave me a sense of fulfillment, a feeling that I had not only adapted to Germany but had embraced it and found a way to create a familiar and new life. This sense of home reminded me that I had risen above the initial challenges and found peace and purpose in a place that had once felt foreign. It was a milestone that represented the culmination of my journey, a moment when I knew I had truly arrived.

These milestone achievements—each representing a significant step forward—were the beacons that illuminated my path, guiding me through the challenges and reminding me of the strength I had cultivated along the way. Each milestone was a reminder that resilience could indeed yield success, that even in the land of shadows, it was possible to rise, to create a life filled with purpose, stability, and fulfillment. These moments were not just achievements; they were a testament to my journey, a reminder that, despite the odds, I had forged a path to success and created a life that was indeed my own.

The Power of Community

The journey of a foreigner in Germany is often challenging, filled with hurdles that can feel isolating and overwhelming. Yet, one of the most significant sources of strength for many of us is the community we build with others who share a similar journey. The foreign community in Germany, comprised of people from all corners of the world, brings a sense of connection, understanding, and mutual support that is invaluable. In a place where many of us feel like outsiders, this community provides a feeling of belonging, a reminder that we are not alone in our experiences. Over time, this community becomes not just a support network but a source of empowerment, as each person's journey strengthens the collective resilience of everyone involved.

Finding the Foreign Community: The First Connections

When I first arrived in Germany, everything felt unfamiliar, from the language to the cultural norms to the structure of everyday life. Despite my determination to adapt, there were days when the feeling of being a stranger in a foreign land weighed heavily. I longed for connection and familiarity, and I first sought out the foreign community in these moments of isolation.

Many foreigners in Germany find their way to each other through language classes, community events, or even social media groups. These initial connections often happen by chance, a shared glance in a crowded room, a friendly greeting in broken German, or a conversation in English or another familiar language. These encounters, simple as they may seem, are the beginnings of friendships that often become lifelines of support.

For me, it was a chance meeting at a local café that led to my first real connection. I met another foreigner from my home country who had lived in Germany for years. He shared his experiences, struggles, and advice for navigating life here. In that conversation, I felt a sense of comfort I hadn't felt since arriving. His insights helped me see that while the challenges were accurate, there was a path forward, and I wasn't alone. That first connection began my journey into the foreign community, a journey that would become an essential part of my life in Germany.

Building Support Networks: Strength in Shared Experiences

As I became more involved in the foreign community, I realized the strength that came from shared experiences. The support networks we built were based on a mutual understanding of the challenges we each faced—language barriers, bureaucratic hurdles, finding work, and navigating the social landscape of Germany. In a way, our community became a place where we could share our frustrations openly, where we didn't have to explain the difficulty of adjusting to an unfamiliar system because everyone understood it firsthand.

These support networks were formed in many ways. Some developed through regular gatherings, where people shared meals, stories, and advice. For others, they were built through online forums and groups, where foreigners posted questions and offered help to those newer to the journey. There was a spirit of generosity and empathy in these networks, a sense that we were all together, each of us lifting the other when things got tough.

In these support networks, I found people who understood the small victories that might seem insignificant to outsiders—successfully navigating a bureaucratic process, securing a stable job, or finally being able to converse in German. Each success was celebrated, not just by the person who achieved it but by the entire community, and these shared moments of progress brought us closer, reminding us that every step forward was worth acknowledging, no matter how small.

Learning and Growing Together: The Role of Mentorship and Guidance

Within the foreign community, mentorship naturally emerged to share knowledge and support one another. Those in Germany for longer often took on a guiding role, sharing what they had learned with newcomers. This mentorship wasn't formal; it was usually as simple as offering advice over a coffee or explaining a bureaucratic process that had confused me. These moments of guidance were invaluable, providing newcomers with the insights they needed to avoid common pitfalls and make their journey a bit easier.

I was fortunate to have mentors within the community who offered advice on everything from job applications to navigating the complexities of the healthcare system. Their guidance saved me time, energy, and frustration, allowing me to focus on building a stable life rather than constantly struggling with each new challenge. This mentorship was one of the most valuable aspects of the foreign community—a form of support beyond friendship, offering practical help that made a real difference in my daily life.

In time, I found myself in a position to mentor others. As I gained experience and confidence, I became one of the people newcomers turned to for advice. Sharing what I had learned was a way of giving back and contributing to the community that had helped me. I realized that mentorship within the foreign community was a cycle where each person's journey could help guide others, creating a collective strength that grew with every shared insight and piece of advice.

Emotional Support: Finding Comfort in Shared Struggles

Living in a foreign country brings not only practical challenges but also emotional ones. The feelings of isolation, homesickness, and self-doubt can be overwhelming, especially in a place where the culture and language are different from what you've known all your life. For many of us, the foreign community became a source of emotional support, where we could express these feelings without fear of judgment or misunderstanding.

I found solace in the friendships I built within the community. We could talk openly about our struggles and share the moments of doubt that came with adapting to a new country. Whether it was a conversation over dinner, a late-night phone call, or a message in an online group, these connections provided a sense of comfort essential to my well-being. Knowing that others had felt the same way, that they understood the unique challenges of our journey, made the difficult moments more bearable.

The emotional support within the foreign community went beyond shared struggles; it also included celebrations of our resilience and achievements. We encouraged each other to keep going, push through the difficult days, and hold onto the hope of a better future. This support was a reminder that while the journey was challenging, it was also filled with growth, strength, and moments of joy. Together, we learned to find peace within the struggle, accept that our journey was valuable and that each challenge was a step toward becoming more robust and resilient.

Creating a Sense of Belonging: Building a Home Away from Home

One of the most powerful aspects of the foreign community was the sense of belonging it created. Many of us had left behind family, friends, and familiar surroundings to start a new life in Germany. The foreign community became a surrogate family, where we found connections that filled the gap left by the loved ones we had left behind. We celebrated holidays, shared meals from home countries, and supported each other during significant life events. These moments created a feeling of home, a reminder that while we were far from our roots, we had built a new family in each other.

This sense of belonging was significant because many felt like outsiders in the broader German society. The foreign community became a space where we didn't have to explain ourselves, where our backgrounds and experiences were understood without needing explanation. It was a place where our differences were celebrated, and our cultures, languages, and traditions were welcomed and appreciated.

This acceptance allowed us to bring ourselves into the community to share who we were without fear of judgment or exclusion.

Through this sense of belonging, we found a source of strength beyond the practical support we offered each other. We found a place where we could be ourselves and stuck to our deep-seated identities while embracing the journey of adaptation and integration. This duality—of being both foreigners and a part of something larger—created a unique sense of community, a place where we felt both seen and supported.

Empowering Each Other: The Ripple Effect of Success

One of the foreign community's most inspiring aspects was how each person's success created a ripple effect that empowered others. When someone within the community reached a milestone—finding stable work, securing housing, or achieving a personal goal—it wasn't just their victory but a victory for all of us. These successes became symbols of hope, reminders that progress was possible even in the face of adversity.

Seeing others achieve their goals inspired me to keep pushing forward and believe I could overcome my challenges. Each person's journey, each small step toward success, became a source of motivation for everyone in the community. We celebrated each other's achievements, knowing that every victory, no matter how small, was a testament to our resilience and determination.

This ripple effect of success created a culture of encouragement within the community. We lifted each other, offering words of support, practical advice, and the reassurance that we could achieve our goals. This empowerment reminded us that while we each had our journeys, we were also part of something larger: a community of people who believed in each other's potential and were committed to rising together.

Facing Challenges Together: Resilience in the Face of Adversity

The foreign community in Germany is not without its challenges. We faced discrimination, systemic barriers, and moments of despair that could easily have overwhelmed us. But through the power of community, we found the resilience to keep going. Together, we learned to navigate these obstacles, sharing strategies for overcoming our difficulties.

When one of us encountered a setback, the community rallied to offer support, advice, and encouragement. We were able to face adversity with a sense of solidarity, knowing that we had a network of people who would stand by us. This collective resilience became one of the most powerful aspects of our community, a reminder that together, we could face challenges that might have felt impossible to overcome alone.

This resilience was built not only on shared struggles but also on shared hope. We believed in each other's potential, the possibility of a better future, and the strength we each brought to the community. Through this belief, we could rise above the challenges and find a path forward even when the odds seemed stacked against us.

The Lasting Impact of Community: A Source of Lifelong Connection

As the years passed, the connections I made within the foreign community in Germany became more than support networks; they became lifelong friendships, a source of connection that extended beyond the country's borders. Even as some of us moved on to different places or different phases of life, the bond we had built remained strong. The experiences we shared, the challenges we faced, and the successes we celebrated together created a lasting sense of solidarity.

The foreign community in Germany taught me the power of connection, the importance of empathy, and the resilience that comes from supporting one another. It was a reminder that while the journey of adaptation and integration is deeply personal, it is also strengthened by the presence of others who share that journey. The community we built was a testament to the strength of the human spirit, a reminder that together, we can rise above even the most difficult challenges.

Chapter 7
The Devil's Game in the Face of Hypocrisy

NAVIGATING LIFE AS a foreigner in Germany meant learning to recognize and endure the hypocrisy in certain aspects of society. On the surface, Germany is a place that champions equality, opportunity, and inclusiveness. But, like many places, beneath this polished image lay a complex web of contradictions—a devil's game, if you will, where rules were often not what they seemed. As I pushed forward, trying to build a life for myself, I found that these double standards sometimes made the journey even more challenging.

This chapter is about confronting the reality of those double standards—the expectations of foreigners to adapt without full inclusion, the economic structures that seem fair but create barriers for outsiders, and the social norms that welcome newcomers but keep them at a distance. In writing this, I aim to reflect openly on how these hidden obstacles affected my journey and the strategies I developed to navigate this game.

Hidden Barriers to Bureaucracy

One of the first places I encountered hypocrisy was within the German bureaucratic system. Germany is known for its strict organization of the thorough and often complicated processes governing everything from registering your address to securing a residence permit. While this orderliness ensures transparency on the surface, it also creates countless barriers for newcomers. Every step forward revealed a new layer of complexity designed to weed out those who couldn't keep up.

Applying for a residence permit was a lesson in patience and persistence. The documents required were exhaustive and specific, and any minor error could set you back weeks if not months. What struck me most was that the system did not seem designed to assist newcomers in understanding or navigating these processes but to test our resilience. Information that should have been straightforward was often buried in legal jargon or made available only through word-of-mouth from those who had already struggled. This approach created a division: those who managed to navigate the bureaucracy successfully and those who remained in the shadows unable to establish a stable life due to misunderstandings or minor missteps.

The hypocrisy lay in the contrast between Germany's reputation as a place of opportunity and the reality of its barriers to entry. A country that celebrated diversity on paper often resisted making its systems accessible to outsiders. For many of us, the devil's game was about patience and relentless persistence, finding ways to outsmart a system that seemed determined to keep us at arm's length.

The Labor Market: A Level Playing Field Only in Theory

The job market was another arena where hypocrisy surfaced. Germany is known for its skilled Industriousness market, where merit and qualifications are supposedly vital to success. Yet, as a foreigner, I quickly learned that there were often unspoken prerequisites to being entirely accepted in the workplace. Job opportunities were there, but they came with invisible strings attached—expectations that you would not only have the technical skills but also a seamless cultural fit.

For many foreigners, the struggle began with having their qualifications recognized. Degrees from other countries often require translation, verification, and sometimes additional study or exams to be considered valid. These extra steps burdened those from abroad, even if they were highly skilled. Ironically, many jobs that required these qualifications were in fields with chronic blue collar worker employment shortages, where one would assume that skills alone would suffice. Yet, the hidden layers of approval meant that foreign workers were often kept out or delayed from joining these professions.

When I finally found a job, I realized that being seen as a cultural outsider created additional pressures. In meetings and daily interactions, I felt the need to prove myself, to avoid making even the slightest mistake, as if one misstep could reinforce stereotypes about foreigners. The pressure to conform while simultaneously standing out was exhausting, a game where the rules were unclear and constantly shifting. It became apparent that fitting in was as important as professional competence, an unspoken expectation that made the playing field anything but level.

Social Expectations: The Illusion of Integration

Germany has long promoted itself as a multicultural society, a place where people from all backgrounds are welcome. But in reality, integration often felt like a one-way street. As foreigners, we were encouraged to adapt, to learn the language, to respect cultural norms—yet full inclusion was rarely extended in return. Social integration was more than just learning German or celebrating Oktoberfest; it was about navigating the boundaries between acceptance and exclusion.

Social gatherings and professional environments revealed this contradiction. While Germans were generally polite and open to new ideas, there were unspoken rules about how far one could integrate without overstepping. Certain social circles remained closed, and while invitations might be extended for public or professional events, the private side of life was often kept off-limits. For many foreigners, this created a sense of isolation, a feeling of always being on the outside looking in. You could participate, but you could never entirely belong.

The hypocrisy of integration policies is that while foreigners are encouraged to assimilate, the unspoken social structures make it difficult to achieve true inclusion. Friendships remained surface-level, and despite all efforts to integrate, I often felt that I was being asked to adjust to fit into spaces where full acceptance was never really on the table. This devil's game of integration required finding a balance between adapting and retaining a sense of self, a challenge few fully prepared us for.

Economic Realities: The Myth of Equal Opportunity

Germany's economic system is built on stability, social welfare, and fairness principles. However, navigating the financial landscape as a foreigner exposed a different reality—where equal opportunity was often a distant ideal. From securing loans to building credit, the financial sector was filled with hidden roadblocks for those without long-standing connections or a local financial history. For many of us, financial stability became a game where the rules applicated locals and established residents.

Accessing credit, for instance, was a frustrating process. Building a credit history in Germany was difficult for newcomers, as the system relied heavily on long-term records and local references. This lack of history meant that even the most minor financial moves, such as renting a flat or securing a business loan, became significant obstacles for someone just starting. Despite my aspirations and financial planning, I quickly learned that specific opportunities were simply out of reach due to an economic system only for those with established roots.

Employment contracts often reinforced this economic disparity. Many foreigners found themselves in temporary or part-time roles, even if they had the qualifications for full-time positions. Contracts were frequently limited in duration, leaving us in perpetual economic insecurity. For those trying to build a stable life, this arrangement created a cycle of dependence, where temporary contracts and limited benefits stunted financial progress. The devil's game in this arena was about finding ways to build financial security on shaky ground, to create stability in a system that offered little support to those on the margins.

Facing Hypocrisy with Resilience and Strategy

Living with this level of contradiction required resilience and strategic thinking. The devil's game could not be avoided; it must be confronted head-on. For many of us, this meant finding creative ways to navigate the hypocrisy while staying true to our goals. We learned to see each barrier as a challenge to be outsmarted and each setback as a chance to sharpen our approach.

I learned to build a support network and connect with others who had faced similar challenges and could offer insights and advice. Mentorship within the foreign community became invaluable, providing a roadmap that helped me understand and navigate the invisible barriers. By pooling resources and sharing experiences, we found ways to create our paths, to turn the devil's game into a test of strategy rather than an insurmountable obstacle.

Learning to work within the system, to recognize when to adapt and when to push back, became essential. I realized that not every battle was worth fighting and that there were times when resilience meant conserving energy and choosing my battles wisely. Focusing on long-term goals and refusing to be discouraged by temporary setbacks allowed me to move forward even when the odds seemed stacked against me.

A Legacy of Change: Transforming the Game for Future Generations

As tricky as the devil's game was, it also served as a source of motivation—a reminder that change was possible and that each step forward contributed to a legacy of resilience for future generations. While frustrating, the hidden barriers and the hypocrisy did not define my journey; they fuel it. With each challenge overcome, I gained a deeper understanding of the system, insights I could share with others, and knowledge that could make the path more accessible for those who would come after me.

In facing these challenges, I began to see myself as a participant and a catalyst for change. By sharing my experiences openly and supporting others on similar journeys, I contributed to a movement, a push toward a more inclusive and transparent society. The devil's game may still exist, but by confronting it and refusing to be defeated, we create a legacy that transforms it, one where future generation can rise above the shadows.

Ultimately, the hypocrisy I faced taught me more than any straightforward path ever could. It taught me resilience, strategy, adaptability, and the importance of community. It showed me that, even in the face of contradictions, there is power in persistence in finding ways to succeed despite the odds. This journey was a test, a game that revealed not only the limitations of the system but also the strength within myself to rise above it.

A Message of Hope

In the journey of adapting to life in a foreign land, it is easy to be overwhelmed by the struggles—the economic uncertainties, the social challenges, and the feeling of constantly needing to prove oneself. Yet, an enduring hope comes from recognizing the impact of each step taken, each challenge overcomes, and each act of persistence. This hope is not just for ourselves but for those who come after us, for future generations who may one day look back and see that the paths we carved out made their journeys smoother. Despite the shadows, the struggles, and the doubts, each small act of resilience contributes to a legacy of possibility, a foundation that others can build upon.

The Power of Persistence: Small Steps Toward Big Changes

Persistence is one of the most potent forces in life, a quality that can turn even the most minor actions into significant achievements over time. Integrating into a new country is filled with obstacles that can feel insurmountable at times, yet each step forward is a victory, no matter how small. Persistence doesn't mean failing; it means keeping going, even when the path is uncertain or the rewards seem distant.

In my journey, there were countless moments when persistence was the only thing I could rely on. The first job rejections, bureaucratic setbacks, and language difficulties could have made me feel defeated. But each time I faced a setback, I reminded myself that every struggle was part of a more extensive process. Each small victory—securing a job, completing a bureaucratic process, or simply having a successful conversation in German—reinforced the idea that progress was possible and that every step, no matter how small, was building toward something more significant.

This persistence was not only a way to overcome obstacles but also a way to create a legacy of resilience. By pushing forward and refusing to let challenges define me, I laid the groundwork for a path others could follow. Every success, every solution, and every moment of strength contributed to a roadmap for future generations, a reminder that persistence can indeed change the course of a journey.

Adaptability: A Key to Thriving in a Changing World

Adaptability is more than just a skill; it's a mindset that allows us to navigate a constantly changing world. As foreigners in a new land, adaptability becomes essential, embracing each new experience with openness and curiosity. Adapting to a new culture, language, and social norms can feel overwhelming. Still, it is also an opportunity to grow and expand our understanding of ourselves and the world around us.

In my journey, adaptability became my greatest ally. I learned to adjust to the rhythm of German life, understand and respect its values, and find ways of merging my identity with the culture I had chosen. This adaptability allowed me to see challenges not as barriers but as opportunities to learn, evolve, and find new paths forward. I realized that by embracing change and being willing to adapt, I could navigate even the most difficult situations with resilience.

Adaptability is a skill that future generations can inherit, a way of approaching life that allows them to thrive no matter where they are or what challenges they face. By learning to adapt, we show those who come after us that it is possible to find balance and build a life that honors where we come from and where we are going. Adaptability is not about losing oneself but expanding, growing into new possibilities, and creating a rich life with roots and wings.

Building a Legacy: The Impact of Every Small Victory

One of the most powerful realizations in my journey was that each small victory was a personal achievement and a contribution to a legacy that would one day support others. Each bureaucratic form completed, each job secured, and each friendship formed was a step toward creating a roadmap that others could follow. It became clear that the struggles I faced and the solutions I found paved the way for future generations who would benefit from the paths I had cleared.

Building this legacy was not about grand gestures or monumental achievements but about the everyday acts of resilience that added up over time. By sharing my experiences with others, offering guidance to newcomers, and contributing to a community that valued mutual support, I became part of a network laying the foundation for a better future. This legacy was about more than individual success; it was about creating a structure of support, a culture of resilience, and a sense of possibility for those who would one day follow in my footsteps.

This legacy is a message of hope, a reminder that each of us can make a difference and that every challenge overcome is a gift to future generations. By rising above our struggles and finding ways to succeed despite adversity, we show those who come after us that a life of fulfillment and stability is possible. This legacy of resilience and adaptability becomes a beacon of hope, a reminder that, despite the shadows, there is always a path forward.

The Role of Community: A Source of Collective Strength

The journey of adaptation and integration is rarely a solitary one. For many of us, the foreign community in Germany became a lifeline, a source of support that sustained us through the most challenging moments. The value of community lies not only in the practical help it provides but in the sense of belonging it creates, a reminder that we are not alone in our journey. Within this community, each person's success contributes to the collective strength, a source of hope that empowers everyone.

Community is not just a network of support; it is a legacy of shared experiences, a structure that future generations can rely on. Building connections, supporting, and celebrating each other's victories create a resilient, adaptable community filled with hope. This community is a message to future generations, a reminder that they will have a place to turn, a network that understands and values their journey.

The power of community is its ability to lift everyone, turn individual successes into collective achievements, and create a sense of unity that transcends cultural differences. This community will be a source of strength for future generations, a reminder that they are not alone but part of something larger than themselves. The legacy of community is a gift of hope, a support structure that will empower each new generation to rise above their challenges.

Hope for Future Generations: The Promise of a Brighter Path

At the heart of this journey is the hope that future generations will have an easier path and that our struggles will serve as stepping stones for those who come after us. This hope is a reminder that every act of persistence, every adaptation, and every moment of resilience contributes to a brighter future. We create hope by showing that it is possible to overcome obstacles and build a life of stability and fulfillment, even in the face of adversity.

This message of hope is not just for ourselves but those who will one day look back and see the paths we carved out. It is for the children of immigrants, the newcomers who will arrive with dreams and uncertainties, and everyone who seeks to build a life in a new land. Our journey, struggles, and successes are a gift to them, a reminder that they can rise above the shadows and create a life of purpose and stability.

Hope is a legacy, a message transcending time and place, a reminder that the challenges we face today will pave the way for a brighter tomorrow. This hope is our gift to the future, a testament to the power of persistence, adaptability, and community. It is a reminder that while the journey may be difficult, it is also filled with possibility, that each step forward brings us closer to a world where everyone has the opportunity to thrive.

Conclusion: Rising Together

In the journey of building a life in Germany, we have learned that persistence, adaptability, and community are not just qualities that help us survive; they are the foundation of hope, the building blocks of a legacy that will support future generations. This journey is a reminder that each struggle, each victory, and each act of resilience contributes to a larger story, a story of people who rose above the shadows and created a path forward.

This message of hope is a call to future generations, a reminder that they are not alone and part of a legacy of strength and resilience. It is a reminder that the path we walked and the challenges we faced were not just for ourselves but for everyone who will follow. Together, we create a world where persistence and adaptability lead to success, community is a source of empowerment, and hope is a gift passed down from generation to generation.

Ultimately, this journey is not just about surviving but rising and creating a life filled with purpose, stability, and fulfillment. It is a testament to the power of hope, a reminder that no matter the journey's difficulty, there is always a path forward, a way to rise above the shadows and build a meaningful and inspiring life.

Reflections from the Shadows

As I look back on my journey, it is a tapestry woven with moments of triumph and times of profound struggle, each experience adding a new layer of resilience, strength, and understanding. Germany has been a place of shadows—of challenges and uncertainties that tested my resolve—but it has also been a place of light, where I found hope, community, and purpose. Through the successes and hard lessons, I have realized that this journey was about more than achieving specific goals; it was about discovering the depth of my strength and learning to embrace my limitations and potential. In these reflections, I share the wisdom gained along the way and insights that I hope will resonate with others navigating similar paths.

1. Embracing Patience: The Strength in Taking Small Steps

One of the most profound lessons I learned was the value of patience. When I first arrived in Germany, I was eager to achieve my goals quickly, to overcome the challenges and secure the stability I had envisioned. But the reality was different. Progress was slow, filled with setbacks and delays, and I often felt frustrated by how little control I had over the pace of my journey. However, as time passed, I realized that patience wasn't just a necessity; it was a strength, a skill that allowed me to navigate uncertainties gracefully.

Each small step forward, each small victory, became a reminder that progress doesn't always happen in leaps and bounds. The journey was not about rushing to the finish line but building a foundation, one step at a time. This patience taught me to value the process and to understand that actual growth often happens slowly, beneath the surface, as we lay down the roots of resilience. I found strength in these moments of patience, learning to trust that each small step led me toward a larger goal, even if the path was not always clear.

2. Adaptability: The Art of Bending Without Breaking

Adapting to a new environment requires more than just learning the language or understanding social norms; it requires a willingness to change, evolve, and let go of rigid expectations. In

Germany, I found myself in situations that challenged my comfort zone, where I had to find new ways of thinking and behaving to navigate the culture and systems around me. At first, this adaptability felt uncomfortable, like I was losing parts of myself to fit into a new Land mine.

But over time, I learned that adaptability was not about losing myself; it was about expanding, about finding new facets of my identity that could thrive in this new environment. This adaptability became a strength, allowing me to bend without breaking to find ways to merge my values with those of my surroundings. I learned to embrace this flexibility to understand that each adaptation was not a compromise but a way of growing my potential. This lesson taught me that adaptability is a lifelong skill that allows us to face new challenges with resilience and creativity.

3. The Importance of Community: Finding Strength in Connection

One of the most valuable lessons I learned was the power of community. The foreign community in Germany became a source of support, understanding, and connection that sustained me through the most challenging moments. I realized that no journey is genuinely solitary and that our strength often comes from the people who walk beside us, share our struggles, and celebrate our successes.

In the foreign community, I found people who understood my journey and offered guidance and encouragement when needed. This sense of connection taught me the importance of building relationships, seeking out people who share similar experiences, and providing support in return. Community became a foundation, a place where I could be vulnerable and find comfort and strength in knowing I was not alone. This lesson reminded me that we are more robust and that each person's journey contributes to a collective resilience that can carry us through even the darkest times.

4. Embracing Duality: Finding Peace in Contradictions

Living as a foreigner in Germany taught me to embrace duality and accept the contradictions that defined my experience. I was both an insider and an outsider, integrated and set apart, rooted in my own culture and open to the culture around me. This duality was often challenging, a reminder of my differences, but it also became a source of strength, a way of finding peace within myself.

I learned that it was possible to hold multiple truths at once, to be part of German society, and to be true to my own identity. This acceptance of duality allowed me to navigate my life with a sense of balance and to understand that I didn't have to choose between two identities. Embracing this duality taught me to live in the in-between spaces, find harmony in the contrasts, and accept that my journey was unique, shaped by my past and present. This lesson of duality became a foundation for my identity, a reminder that I could belong in multiple places and create an authentic and adaptable life.

5. Resilience: The Quiet Power of Persistence

Resilience became one of the most valuable qualities I developed on this journey. Each setback, each rejection, and each moment of self-doubt was an opportunity to cultivate resilience and learn how to keep going even when the path was difficult. Resilience was not unaffected by challenges; it was about learning to rise after each fall and continue moving forward even when the obstacles felt overwhelming.

This resilience was built slowly through each small act of persistence, each choice to keep going despite the odds. I learned that resilience is a quiet strength, a determination that doesn't always make headlines but creates a foundation of inner strength. This lesson taught me that resilience is not a single act; it is a daily commitment, a way of approaching life with the belief that each challenge is an opportunity to grow. Resilience became my anchor, a reminder that I had the strength to face the journey no matter how difficult.

6. Financial Independence: The Freedom to Rely on Oneself

Achieving financial stability in Germany was a milestone that taught me the importance of independence. For a long time, financial insecurity was a constant source of anxiety, a reminder of the uncertainty that came with living in a foreign land. But as I built my career and learned to budget and save, I found freedom in knowing I could rely on myself and had the resources to create a stable life.

This financial independence was more than just a practical achievement; it was a source of confidence, a reminder that I could build a life of stability and security. This lesson taught me that independence is not just about financial stability but about creating a self-sufficient life where I can choose based on my values and aspirations. This economic independence became a foundation, a source of peace that allowed me to focus on my personal growth and goals.

7. Humility: Learning to Accept Help

One of the hardest lessons to learn was the importance of humility, of accepting that I couldn't do everything alone. At times, I felt a need to prove myself, to show that I could navigate life in Germany without relying on others. However, as the challenges grew, I realized that humility was not a weakness but a strength, a way of recognizing that accepting help is part of the journey.

Through this humility, I learned to lean on the support of friends, mentors, and the community around me. I discovered that asking for help was not a sign of failure but a way of building relationships and connecting with others who understood my journey. This lesson taught me that we are all interdependent and that strength comes not only from independence but from the ability to reach out and accept the support of others. This humility allowed me to grow, accept my limitations, and appreciate the value of community.

8. Legacy: Creating a Path for Others

As I look back on my journey, I realize that each challenge I faced, and each success I achieved was not just for myself but for those who would come after me. I began to see my journey as part of a more significant legacy, a path others could follow, a reminder that it is possible to rise above the shadows and create a life of purpose and fulfillment. This sense of legacy gave my journey a deeper meaning, a reminder that each lesson learned contributed to a brighter future.

This legacy was not about grand achievements; it was about the small acts of resilience, the moments of kindness, and the willingness to help others who were beginning their journey. I learned that legacy is not about what we achieve for ourselves but what we create for others, the paths we clear, the support we offer, and the hope we inspire. This lesson taught me that each of us has the power to make a difference and leave a legacy that empowers future generations to dream, strive, and succeed.

Conclusion: Rising from the Shadows with Wisdom and Strength

Reflecting on this journey, I am grateful for the lessons I have learned, the resilience I have developed, and the community that supported me. The support and encouragement from others played a significant role in my personal growth. Germany has been a place of both challenge and opportunity, where I rose from the shadows to create a life filled with purpose, strength, and hope.

These lessons are not just reflections on the past; they are foundations for the future, reminders that each challenge is an opportunity to grow and success is a step toward building a life of meaning and fulfillment. This journey has taught me that life is rarely straightforward and is often filled with light and shadow, but within each experience, there is wisdom to be gained, strength to be discovered, and hope to be shared. Remember, no matter how challenging the journey, resilience, and hope can always light the way.

Advice to Future Hustlers

To those of you considering a journey like this or who may already be on the path, let me first say this: you are stronger and more capable than you might imagine. Choosing to build a life in a new country is one of the bravest, most challenging things a person can do. You'll face moments of doubt, frustration, and uncertainty, but you'll also find strength, resilience, and joy in places you never expected. This advice is for you, the future hustlers, the dreamers, and the doers as you forge your path.

1. Start with a Clear Vision, But Stay Flexible

One of the most important things you can bring on this journey is a clear vision of what you want to achieve. This vision will be your anchor, your source of motivation during tough times. It might be a vision of financial independence, a career goal, or simply a dream of creating a stable life in a place that offers opportunity. Define your "why" and hold it close.

However, understand that flexibility is just as important as vision. Life will throw unexpected challenges and opportunities your way, and adapting will be essential. Your original vision might change as you grow, learn, and encounter new possibilities. That's okay. Embrace these changes, and remember that flexibility doesn't mean losing sight of your goals—it means finding new ways to reach them. A flexible approach will keep you resilient and open to growth, helping you find success in ways you may not have anticipated.

2. Patience and Persistence Are Your Greatest Allies

Building a life in a new country is a marathon, not a sprint. Patience and persistence are your greatest allies, keeping you going when progress feels slow or obstacles seem insurmountable. There will be days, months, or even years when you're barely moving forward. Remember that every small step matter and that each persistence day adds up during these times.

Set small, achievable goals and celebrate each one. Whether completing a German language course, securing your first job, or navigating a bureaucratic process, each achievement is a milestone on your journey. Persistence isn't about never failing but continuing despite the failures. Trust that every effort is part of the bigger picture and that, with time, you will see the fruits of your hard work.

3. Invest in Learning the Language and Culture

Language is one of the most powerful tools in a new country. Invest time and energy in learning the language of your new home, even if it feels difficult. Language skills will open doors, make daily life more accessible, and help you build deeper connections with the people around you. More importantly, it will give you confidence and independence, allowing you to navigate the culture quickly.

But learning a language is just the beginning. Take time to understand the culture, the unspoken social norms, and the values that shape the society you're entering. This knowledge will help you avoid misunderstandings, build respect, and show others you're committed to integrating. Embracing the local culture doesn't mean abandoning your own—it means creating a bridge between where you come from and where you're going. This cultural understanding will be one of your greatest assets, allowing you to navigate life with respect, confidence, and authenticity.

4. Don't Be Afraid to Ask for Help

In a new country, you'll encounter challenges you may not know how to face alone. This is where humility and community come into play. Don't be afraid to ask for help, whether it's guidance on bureaucracy, advice on finding housing, or simply companionship in times of loneliness. Asking for help isn't a sign of weakness; it's a recognition of your complex journey and a way of connecting with others who have walked similar paths.

Seek out networks, communities, and mentors who can offer support. Many people in the foreign community understand precisely what you're going through and are often willing to share their knowledge and experience. Building these connections will make your journey easier and give you a sense of belonging, a feeling that you're not alone. Remember that we all need help sometimes, and each person you meet has something valuable to offer.

5. Create a Financial Plan and Stick to It

Financial stability is one of the most empowering things you can achieve on this journey. From the start, create a realistic financial plan that covers your basic needs and includes savings, even if initially modest. Stick to this plan as much as possible and make financial decisions with a long-term perspective. Building a stable life requires patience and discipline, especially when finances are uncertain.

Avoid unnecessary debts, save wherever you can, and be mindful of your spending habits. Remember that building financial stability is a process, one that requires careful planning and sacrifice at times. Financial independence will allow you to choose what's best for you rather than being tied down by financial limitations. This economic foundation is essential to creating a secure, fulfilling life.

6. Adaptability Is the Key to Overcoming Challenges

Adaptability will be your superpower in a new country. Life won't always go according to plan, and you'll encounter unexpected, confusing, or frustrating situations. Adaptability allows you to find new solutions, adjust your approach, and stay resilient when the path is unclear. This ability to pivot to see challenges as opportunities for growth will be invaluable.

Learn to see change as a chance to grow and find new strengths within yourself. Adaptability doesn't mean compromising your values; it means finding ways to reach your goals by embracing new methods, ideas, and perspectives. With adaptability, you'll find yourself more prepared to handle life's ups and downs, more willing to explore new possibilities, and more confident in your ability to thrive no matter what comes your way.

7. Build and Lean on a Support Network

Creating a support network is essential to your well-being and success. This journey is too challenging to undertake alone, and the connections you build with others will provide strength, comfort, and guidance. Seek out communities, friends, and mentors who understand your experience, can offer advice, and are willing to listen when things get tough.

These relationships will become some of your most valuable resources. They'll remind you that you're not alone, that others are facing similar struggles, and that there's always someone who can lend a helping hand. A support network isn't just about receiving help; it's also about giving back and building a community where everyone can thrive together. You'll grow more robust, connected, and empowered to support others.

8. Find Moments of Joy and Celebrate Small Wins

In the hustle to achieve your goals, it's easy to overlook the importance of joy and celebration. Life in a new country will come with its fair share of hardships, but it brings moments of happiness, discovery, and connection. Find joy in the small things—a successful conversation in a new language, a friendship made, a cultural experience that feels meaningful.

Celebrate your wins, no matter how small they may seem. Recognize each achievement, each step forward, as a testament to your strength and determination. These moments of joy and celebration will sustain you, reminding you of your progress and giving you the energy to keep moving forward. Life is not just about the destination; it's about finding meaning and fulfillment in the journey.

9. Embrace Resilience: Learn to Rise After Every Fall

Resilience is what will carry you through the most challenging times. There will be moments of failure when you feel discouraged or uncertain about your path. In these moments, remember that resilience isn't about avoiding challenges; it's about learning to rise after every fall. It's about recognizing that setbacks are part of the journey and that each failure is a chance to learn, grow, and return stronger.

Cultivate a mindset of resilience by focusing on your strengths, finding solutions even when they're not immediately apparent, and reminding yourself of your purpose. Resilience will help you face challenges with determination, knowing that each obstacle is an opportunity to develop the skills, wisdom, and strength needed to succeed. Embrace resilience, and remember that every setback is just one step in reaching your goals.

10. Leave a Legacy for Future Hustlers

Finally, remember that your journey is part of a more significant legacy. Each success you achieve, each obstacle you overcome, is not only for yourself but for those who will come after you. Please share your experiences, offer guidance to newcomers, and contribute to the community in ways that make it easier for others to follow in your footsteps.

Leaving a legacy means giving back, creating a path that others can walk with greater ease, and knowing that you've already cleared some obstacles. By supporting others, you make a ripple effect that extends beyond your journey, positively impacting future generations of hustlers, dreamers, and doers. Your story, journey, and successes will inspire others, giving them the courage and hope they need to pursue their dreams.

In Closing

To all the future hustlers: this journey will not be easy, but it will be worth it. Each challenge you face and each victory you achieve is a testament to your strength, resilience, and commitment to building a better life. Trust yourself, stay true to your vision, and know that you are part of a legacy of individuals who dared to pursue their dreams, no matter the odds.

"If there is one thing, I learned that no matter how good you are, you can never be good enough for another man who is not ready to be a man."

About the Author

Willy Lapse Laguerre is more than just an author—he is a storyteller, a cultural navigator, and an entrepreneur with a mission to inspire and uplift others through his life experiences. Born in the Caribbean and raised in Key West, he ventured far from his roots to pursue new opportunities, dreams, and a purpose-filled life in Germany. His journey is a testament to resilience, determination, and the power of community, as he transformed the many challenges of living abroad into a legacy of hope, wisdom, and encouragement for those who come after him.

With a professional background as a motivator, fashion designer, entrepreneur, and author, Willy Lapse Laguerre has worn many hats throughout his life. His versatility is not just a skill but a necessity he embraced while adapting to new environments. Each role he took was a step in a broader journey of self-discovery, adaptation, and growth. His work spans motivational writing, children's literature, and social themes, reflecting his dedication to exploring life's most profound questions, values, and complexities.

In his inspiring memoir *Where the Shadow Cannot Reach*, Willy Lapse Laguerre recounts his experiences with courage, authenticity, and a keen eye for life's paradoxes. He shares the challenges of adjusting to a foreign land, facing economic obstacles, and navigating cultural divides while building a life of meaning in Germany. His insights into the resilience required to succeed abroad and the strategies he used to turn obstacles into stepping stones are valuable lessons for anyone seeking to rise above their circumstances. With each page, he invites readers into his world, offering a window into the life of a determined hustler who learned to thrive despite the odds.

One of his most famous works, *The Forbidden Love,* delves into themes of cultural differences, romance, social experimentation, and cultural shock. Through this book, Willy Lapse Laguerre explores love's complexities that defy conventions, offering readers a deeply personal and universally relatable story. His sensitivity to cultural nuances and human emotions is evident throughout the narrative, reflecting his ability to capture the beauty and challenges of relationships that bridge worlds.

As a father and author of multiple children's books, Willy Lapse Laguerre also aims to inspire young minds through tales of adventure and discovery. His children's stories are designed to cultivate curiosity, resilience, and an appreciation for diversity. Each story encourages young readers to explore the world around them and see life's obstacles as opportunities for growth. For Willy Lapse Laguerre, writing for children is an extension of his journey, a way of passing on the wisdom he has gained and empowering the next generation to dream big and embrace life's adventures.

A theme that runs through much of his work is the power of adaptation and resilience—a message he hopes to expand in his upcoming book, *The Art of Ignorance to Live Happily*. In this book, Willy Lapse Laguerre will explore the value of selective focus, a skill he believes is essential in today's world, where information, pressures, and expectations constantly bombard people. Through thoughtful anecdotes, research insights, and reflective exercises, he intends to guide readers toward a life of mindfulness, peace, and contentment by embracing the art of knowing less and living more fully.

Willy Lapse Laguerre is also working on a memoir about his life as a determined hustler in Germany, a journey marked by paradoxes and economic challenges. In this work, he aims to shed light on the unique experiences of foreigners in Germany, sharing the financial hurdles, social dynamics, and cultural adjustments they must navigate to establish a stable life. Through raw truth and a touch to the frame of mind, he reflects on how even the "shadows" of a society can shape a person's resilience and creativity. His reflections aim to inspire readers who face similar journeys, reminding them that even in the most challenging environments, one can find purpose, fulfillment, and a sense of belonging.

At the core of Willy Lapse's work is a deep commitment to building community and leaving a legacy for those who come after him. His writing is not just a personal artistic core but a way of giving back, offering guidance and hope to those who walk similar paths. As someone who has lived the experience of starting from scratch in a foreign country, he understands the importance of resilience, adaptability, and support. His books reflect his belief that everyone has the power to rise above their circumstances, build a life of meaning, and make a difference in the lives of others.

Through his storytelling, Willy Lapse Laguerre invites readers of all ages to see beyond their immediate challenges, embrace the possibilities within their journey, and believe in their ability to create positive change. His work is a call to action, a reminder that resilience is not just about surviving but about thriving, finding joy in the journey, and leaving a legacy that others can build upon. Whether he is writing for children, adults, or fellow hustlers, his message is clear: life is a journey of growth, and with courage, patience, and community, each of us has the power to shape our destiny.

For Willy Lapse Laguerre, writing is more than just a profession; it is a purpose, a way of reaching out to others, and a means of creating a lasting impact. As he continues to expand his body of work, he remains dedicated to inspiring readers to live fully, embrace diversity, and see each challenge as an opportunity for growth. His journey from his homeland to Germany, from uncertainty to stability, from struggle to success, serves as a reminder that dreams are attainable, that obstacles can be overcome, and that hope is a powerful force for change.

With every book, Willy Lapse Laguerre leaves a piece of himself, a glimpse into his heart and his hard-won wisdom, creating a legacy that will resonate for generations. His life is a testament to the power of persistence, the importance of community, and the beauty of building a life with an ultimate goal, one's roots and the dreams that drive us forward. Through his stories, he offers readers the courage to pursue their journeys, rise above their shadows, and create lives rich with purpose, passion, and possibility.

Don't miss out!

Visit the website below and you can sign up to receive emails whenever Willy Lapse Laguerre publishes a new book. There's no charge and no obligation.

https://books2read.com/r/B-A-QNFNC-GFVHF

BOOKS 2 READ

Connecting independent readers to independent writers.

Did you love *A Hustler's Journey - Against The Shadow*? Then you should read *The Game You Can Never Win*[1] by Willy Lapse Laguerre!

[2]

Summary and Reflections

This journey explored the essential elements needed to form deep and meaningful connections. We discussed how setting clear intentions can lay a strong foundation for trust and authenticity in relationships. By practicing active engagement, like listening carefully and showing genuine interest, we can make others feel valued and respected. Embracing vulnerability is also crucial; opening up and sharing personal experiences allows for a more profound understanding and empathy between individuals. Revisiting meaningful conversations ensures relationships remain dynamic and adaptable to change, providing opportunities to address unresolved issues and celebrate

---

1. https://books2read.com/u/bOqNpK

2. https://books2read.com/u/bOqNpK

progress. Looking ahead, it's clear that relationships thrive on consistency and openness. Regular communication acts as the lifeline connecting partners, fostering a sense of trust and mutual respect. Being transparent and accountable reinforces our commitment to the relationship, making each partner feel secure. Celebrating shared milestones and embracing diverse perspectives further enriches the connection, adding layers of depth and understanding. Cultivating satisfying connections requires patience and dedication, like tending to a growing plant. Investing time and effort while respecting individuality creates an environment where relationships can flourish authentically and robustly.

to reconsider their approaches to competition, ambition, and life's uncertain journey.

Milton Keynes UK
Ingram Content Group UK Ltd.
UKHW021841231124
451423UK00001B/166

9 798224 032778